```
COULTER LIBRARY ONONDAGA COMM. COLL.
PS3559.I8 N3
Wilhelm, Fritz. Next step
```
3 0418 00008614 8

```
PS
3559
.I8      Wilhelm, Fritz
N3
         Next step.
```

DATE DUE			

```
HEISING, M. AND WILHE 00/00/00
NEXT STEP
(5) 1982 DUP-PS3559.I8N3
0165  01 808789  01 1    (IC=0)
```
B016501808789011B

SIDNEY B. COULTER LIBRARY
Onondaga Community College
Syracuse, New York 13215

NEXT STEP

THE SIDNEY B. COULTER LIBRARY
ONONDAGA COMMUNITY COLLEGE
RTE 173, ONONDAGA HILL
SYRACUSE, NEW YORK 13215

Poems: *Fritz Wilhelm*
Linocuts: *Margrete Heising*

NEXT STEP

Published by

Margrete Heising   and
Fritz Wilhelm
1298 Windermere Way
Concord, Ca. 94521

Distributed by

Alchemy Books
681 Market St. #755
S. F., CA 94105

and by M. Heising and F. Wilhelm

International Standard Book Number 0-931290-57-0

© 1981 by Margrete Heising and Fritz Wilhelm. All rights in all countries reserved. No part
of this book may be translated, reproduced or used in any form or by any means whatsoever without permission.

Limited first edition (2,000 copies)

printed by Economy Bookcraft, San Francisco, California

INTRODUCTION

We feel that the essence of a human being is unfathomable. Clearly in our society this aspect of man has become increasingly overshadowed by his scientific superstition on one hand and by a so-called demythologizing of religion and art on the other. An attitude is spreading in which anything that cannot be explained through formal reason and logic is looked upon as irrelevant or even nonsensical. The reaction to this attitude is unfortunately a belief in the irrational and nonsensical. The result of these two complimentary approaches to life in general is quite naturally confusion, despair, and cynicism.

Art has all too often become an intellectual and arbitrary game governed by the rules of mass market profits and played by egocentric tricksters. A work of art becomes primarily a marketable product whose success is determined by the ability of the sales people to advertise and package it. For example, poetry, one of the oldest art forms of man, tends to become a game of words and accidental associations, a game which soon computers will be better at than man himself.

What is lost in all this is the depth of the human being, which can only be hinted at by words like love, soul, intelligence, insight, and so forth. It is this area which escapes cogent knowledge but which is determining the very nature of man and woman. We feel that it is in the nature of art, poetry, philosophy, and religion to try to reveal some aspects of this unfathomable essence of man. This act of revelation can of course not be a one-sided, static affair of the artist or philosopher, but rather some kind of communication between a giving and a receiving human being, where giving and receiving become mutual. In this movement between two persons, a movement which is unpredictable, what is true may reveal itself for a fleeting moment. It should be the honest endeavor of an artist — and any human being — to make such moments possible.

It is our hope that this little book can speak in this sense to another human being and appeal to our common "source" which transcends any word and any image.

Fritz Wilhelm
Margrete Heising
Winter 1982

BIOGRAPHICAL NOTES:

MARGRETE HEISING

Margrete Heising was born and raised in Copenhagen, Denmark, where she received her formal art education at the School of Arts and Crafts as illustrator and commercial artist. After her graduation in 1960 she worked in this field in Switzerland. In 1961 she became an art teacher in Copenhagen.

Since the age of twelve she has been painting in oil; her interest in linocut came a few years later. However, in both areas she developed her own style without a teacher or school. From 1970 to 1976 she exhibited her work in several galleries in Copenhagen and received assignments for book- and bookcover illustrations.

In the spring of 1977 she emigrated to California with her husband. Until 1980 she worked as an art teacher in a private school. In the fall of 1981 she moved to Concord where she has been continuing her work as an independent artist.

FRITZ WILHELM

Fritz Wilhelm was born and raised in West Germany where he graduated from the Gymnasium in 1964. Studies of chemistry at the University of Karlsruhe, mathematics and physics at the Sorbonne followed. Master's and Ph.D. degrees from the University of Karlsruhe, West Germany, in theoretical physics.

Breaking away from the university life he spent a year in Oaxaca, Mexico, and Guatemala writing poetry.

In 1974 he met J. Krishnamurti in Saanen, Switzerland, who invited him to come to the United States to start an Adult Educational Center in Ojai, California. He moved there in 1977 with his wife Margrete Heising. Until 1981 he worked in the Adult Center. He explored the deeper issues of life and was influenced by Karl Jaspers, J. Krishnamurti, David Bohm and Kant.

In 1981 he and his wife moved to the bay area of San Francisco, where he lectures in physics, mathematics, and philosophy.

Presently, a book on the "Evolution of Realities" is under work.

NEXT STEP

No—thing—

    IS—

        God—

            One.

Beginning—

    And no time—

        Movement—

            And no space.

Creation and destruction—

    Birth—

        Out of itself—

            Another and another.

Three—

    Moving together

        Creating laws

            Time and space and matter

                Mind

                    A world.

Thought awaking

    To the world

        In a slumber

            As different.

Tree of Life and Death

We want to follow
Like sheep the shepherd,
The Master
Who promises the light,
Who whips us, beats us down,
Grants us rights
With soothing voice,
The vessel of the Gods.
We want to believe
That he is like God—
Our belief—
Who knows and sees
It all.
We want to hope
That he is on our side.

We want to know
The mysteries of Earth and Sky,
Of love and beauty,
And of the budding rose.
We want to touch and smell,
Grasp with our hands,
Or books or brains
The Whole, forever,
To feel so deadly safe, we,
The masters of the universe,
Who know and see
It all—
Our belief—
We want to hope
That knowledge is on our side.

We fear life!
The ever unknown mystery,
The scream of war, of love, of ecstacy.
We fear the baby
With his sea-deep eyes of wisdom,
Ourselves.
We fear the flower
Blooming in its silent blue.
Out of fear—we want to know.
Out of fear—we want to follow and we hope.

Life on Earth

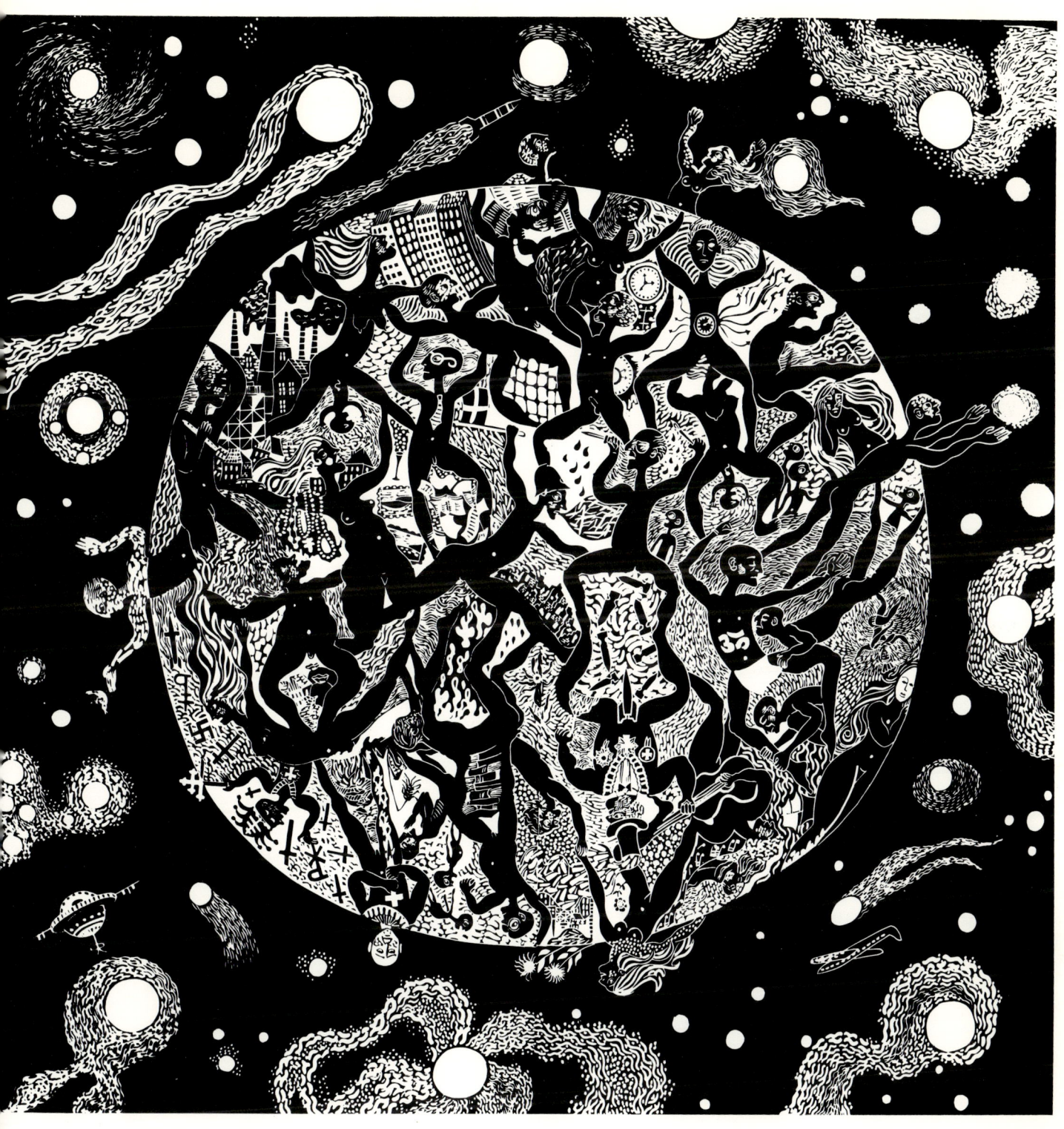

With trembling hearts

Captive like a bird

We find ourselves

Unknown in an unknown world

Of colors, fleeting

Shapes of being.

Words are forming,

Forming worlds,

Fixed,

Like floating rings

Of pebbles

Dropped into the stillness

Of the river by a

Casual hand.

Circles, centered

In the moment of an I,

Moving past majestic mountains

Smiling to

The river's

Fleeting worlds

Of man's imagination.

Reflections

Thoughts are shadows of ideas.

        You look at shadows only,

      Shadow you become.

The idea to see,

The light must see

      Yourself

Casting the shade.

Confusion

Man perfected?

Accomplished?

Becoming, better

From here to there

From yesterday to morrow?

        The tree

        Is

        Seed,

        Roots and trunk and branches,

        Growing, moving---

        Part of larger moving

        And of smaller---

        Leaves and flowers,

        Air and rain and salt,

        Forming, veiling and forgoing---

        and creating.

Man,

Ignorant in stupor,

Moving himself,

Moved and mover,

Wants to become,

To know and measure

Himself,

The trees and seeds

And All---

And does not understand.

Fragmentation

Chained in knowledge

And belief

Of hope and of desire

Man

Fearful

Ploughing barren

Soils of yesterday,

Treads burdened

The iron path

Into an ever promised land.

Burdened

For many a man

Life is without beauty

Or a healing dream.

Life is struggle,

Money, power, pain, conceit.

Some people think they know,

And they explain it all,

Others hope,

And they have their Holy Book.

They have escaped the tapestry of life

And death

And the flowing of a crystal river,

The beauty of the woman, young and old,

The fading of an autumn leaf.

The eyes of a young child.

Isolation

I am,

And the sun is shining,

And I feel the sun,

And her warmth

And her colors,

And war is in the East,

And war is in the West,

And the sun is shining,

And man loves,

And man hates,

And the sun is shining,

And a baby is born,

And a mother dies,

And her children cry,

And the sun is shining,

And I am born,

And I am,

And I die,

And the sun is shining.

And the sun is shining

Whales

Are singing songs

For friends.

The eagle warns.

A seedling grows

Through rocky soil.

But a mother's tears

Taste bitter

In the crowd's applause.

Tears

In your village

People love and hate

And hope and die.

The stars above

They twinkle, shine

And spark and spy

Into your heart

Of sorrow and of joy.

You see the sun,

Piercing through the clouds,

Reach out, to help,

To warm the soil,

The waters, skies of

Your village of

The world.

Your village

Red role dunes

Of rock and sand

Under the blue silence

Of a crystal sky.

The wind sends

Thirsty shivers

Through thorny leaves

Of forlorn grass.

A rattler,

Showing off his

Floating colors

In secret loveplay

With the sand.

A shepherd's silhouette,

Porous waves

Of heat and light,

And solitude.

Song of a serpent

Birds are singing

Flying high

In new born skies

Of fertile blue.

Brooks are murmuring again

Their soothing songs

In moss and fern

Embracing swiftly silver trouts.

Flowers weave anew

Their tapestry in grass,

Resting place

For curious eyes of fawns.

Spring

Lazy spiders resting

In their webs.

Tumble weeds

Roll over fences.

The searing sun

Protects the desert.

Gives life

And kills.

The rattler sleeps

Under shady rocks

Waiting

For the night.

Seeds are falling

Spiders flying

In the waking wind.

Trees get ready

In sogging rain

For rest.

Leaves change colors

Yellow brown and red

And tumble to the ground.

Rivers now run cool

With morning fog

Disguising trees and bushes

Against a weak'ning sun.

Autumn

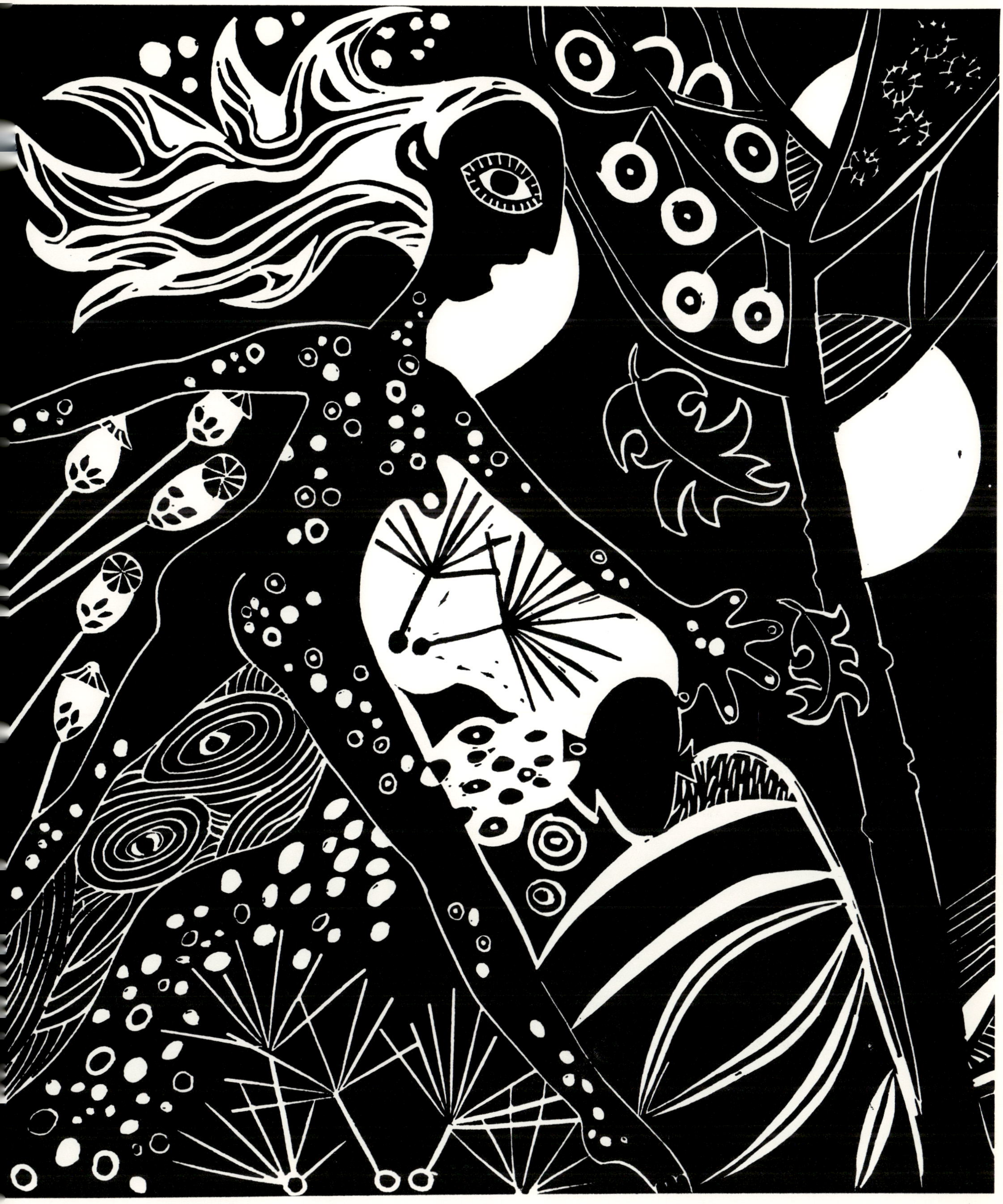

The air is clear

And brilliant

Like a starlit night.

Frost strikes still

And kills,

Starves animals

And man and plants.

Fertile ground

Impenetrable rock,

Frozen to the depth

Of slumbering life.

Winter

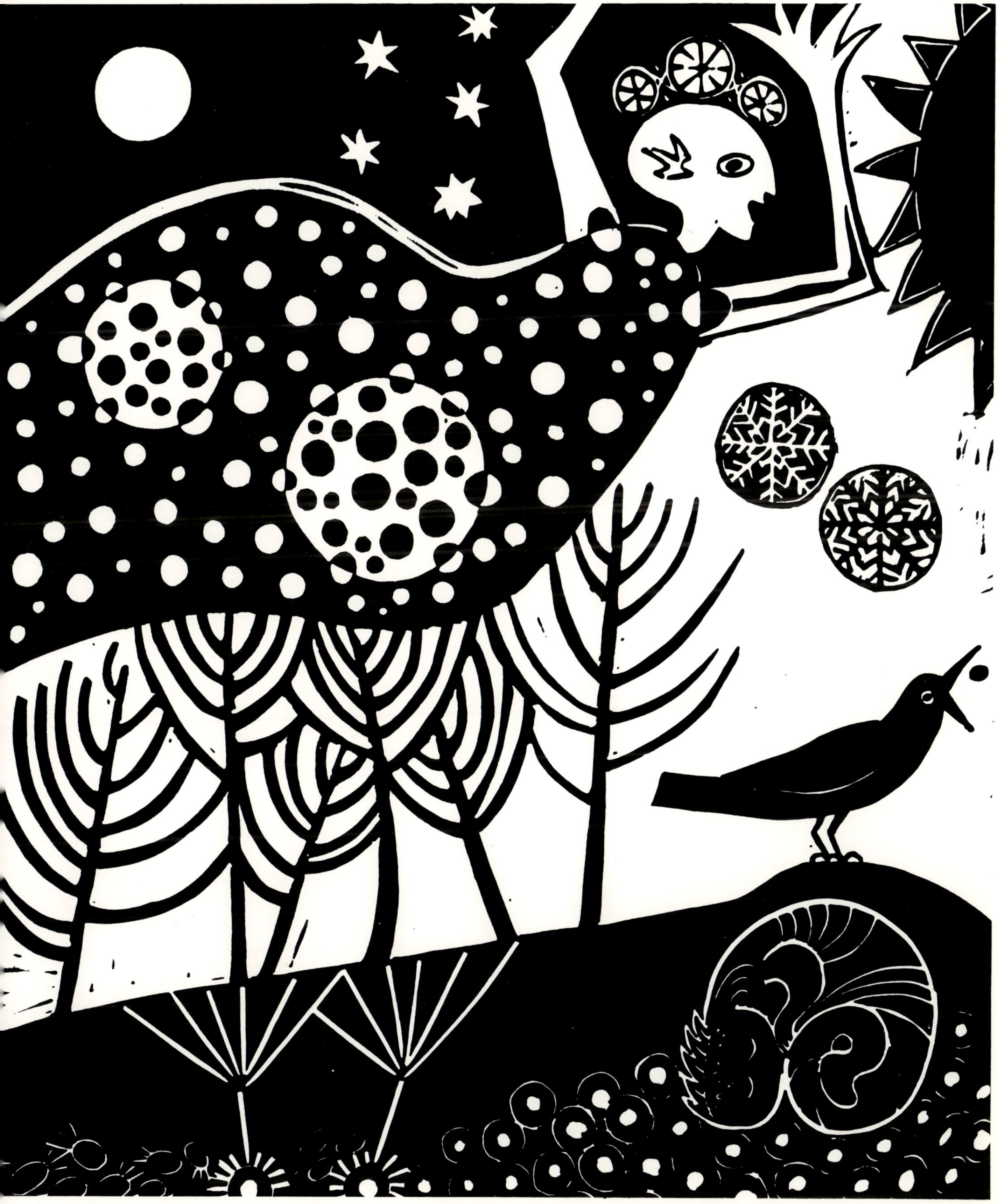

Love is

Of trust

Woven

By unseen hands

And thoughts,

The cloak of wisdom

And of strength,

Beyond knowing,

Yet giving

And demanding

All your heart

And trust

And you.

Friends

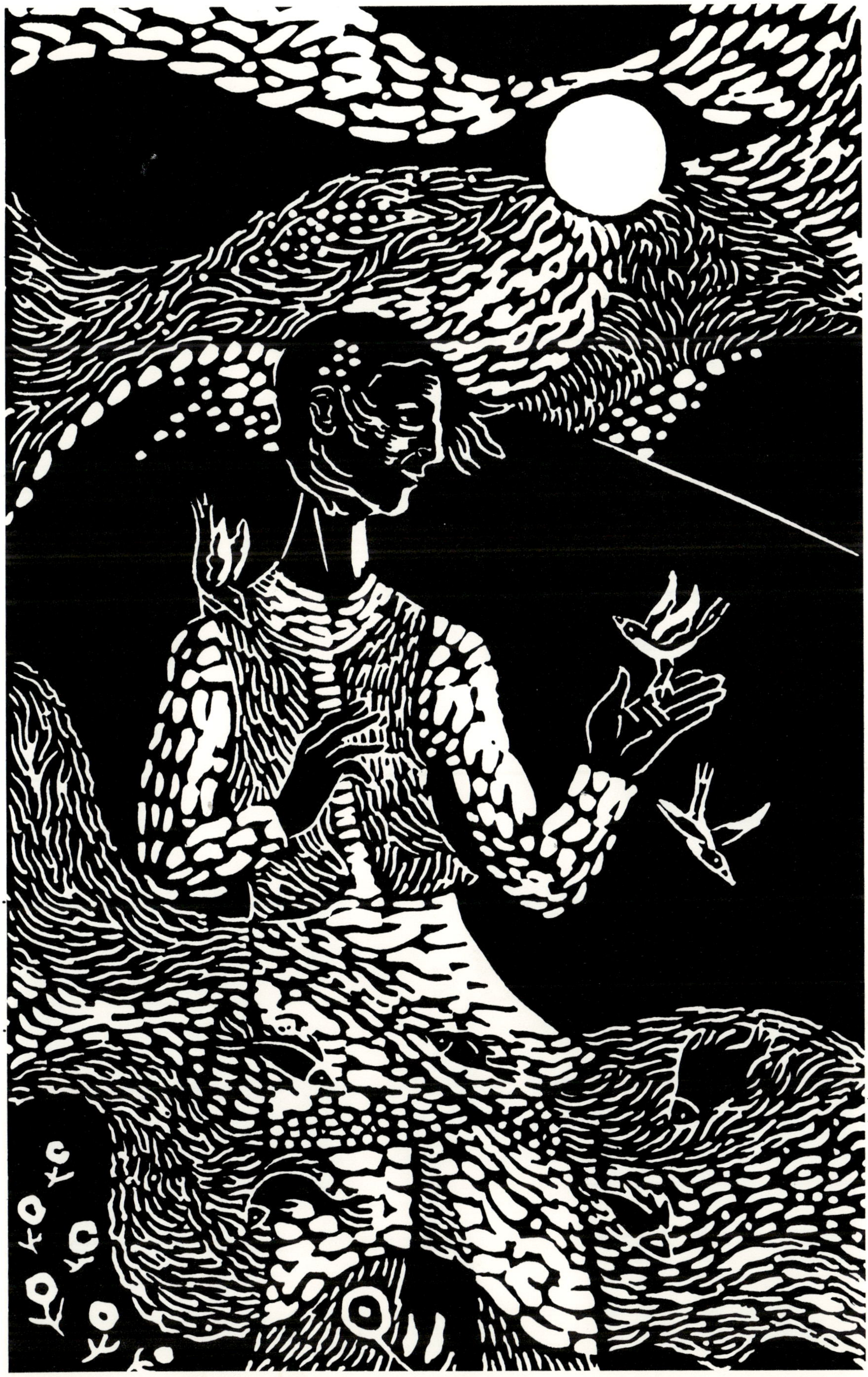

Follow me

My friend

Flowers to collect

In the meadow

Of our life,

Where rivers flow

Together and apart,

To reach the deep-blue ocean

Of love and joy,

Of life together

With a friend.

Follow me

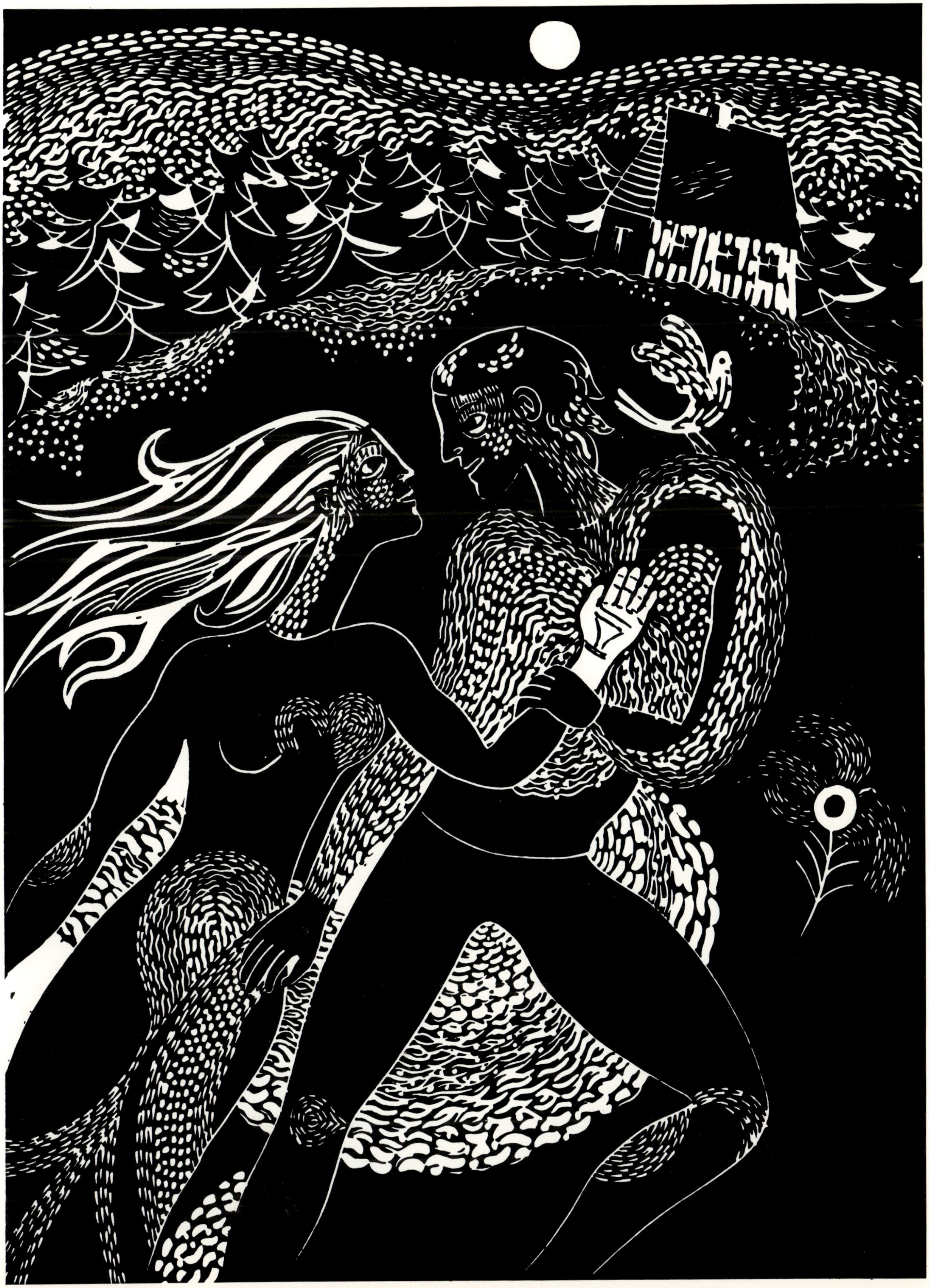

Singing, down the road,

Between hill and vale,

Drowned in the divine,

Arm in arm with happiness,

Praising Gods

Dionysos and Isis,

Loving them with fleeting souls.

Colorful and warm,

White and black and red.

Her mouth, her thighs,

Limbs of cooling fire,

Moving,

Gently,

Like the furious ocean,

Floating, drowning.

Melting, moulding,

Dying.

All and one,

And giving birth,

To a new day.

Alone - together

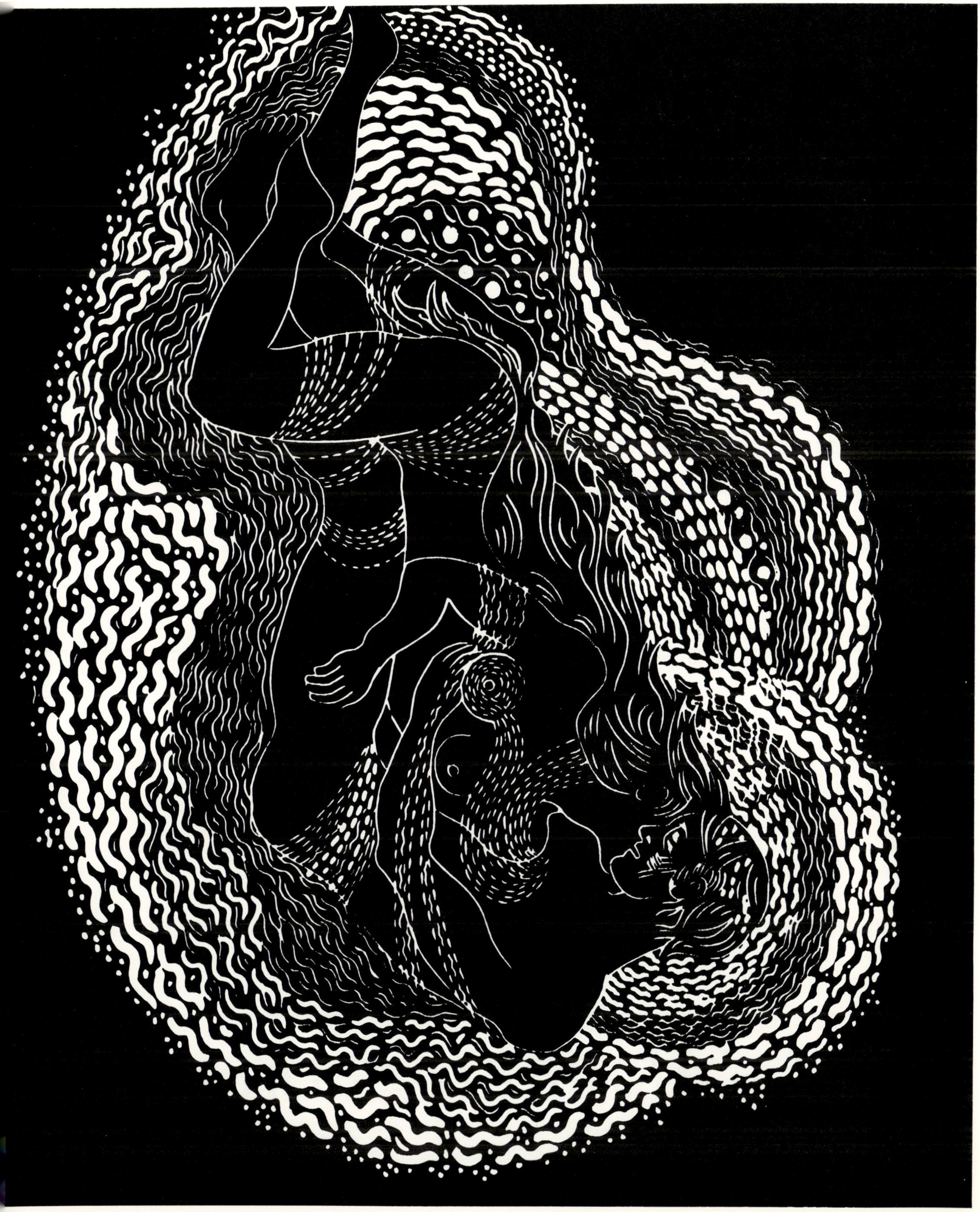

Alive
        Unseen

        Unknown

        Unthought

Timeless

God and

Love.

"I am that I am"

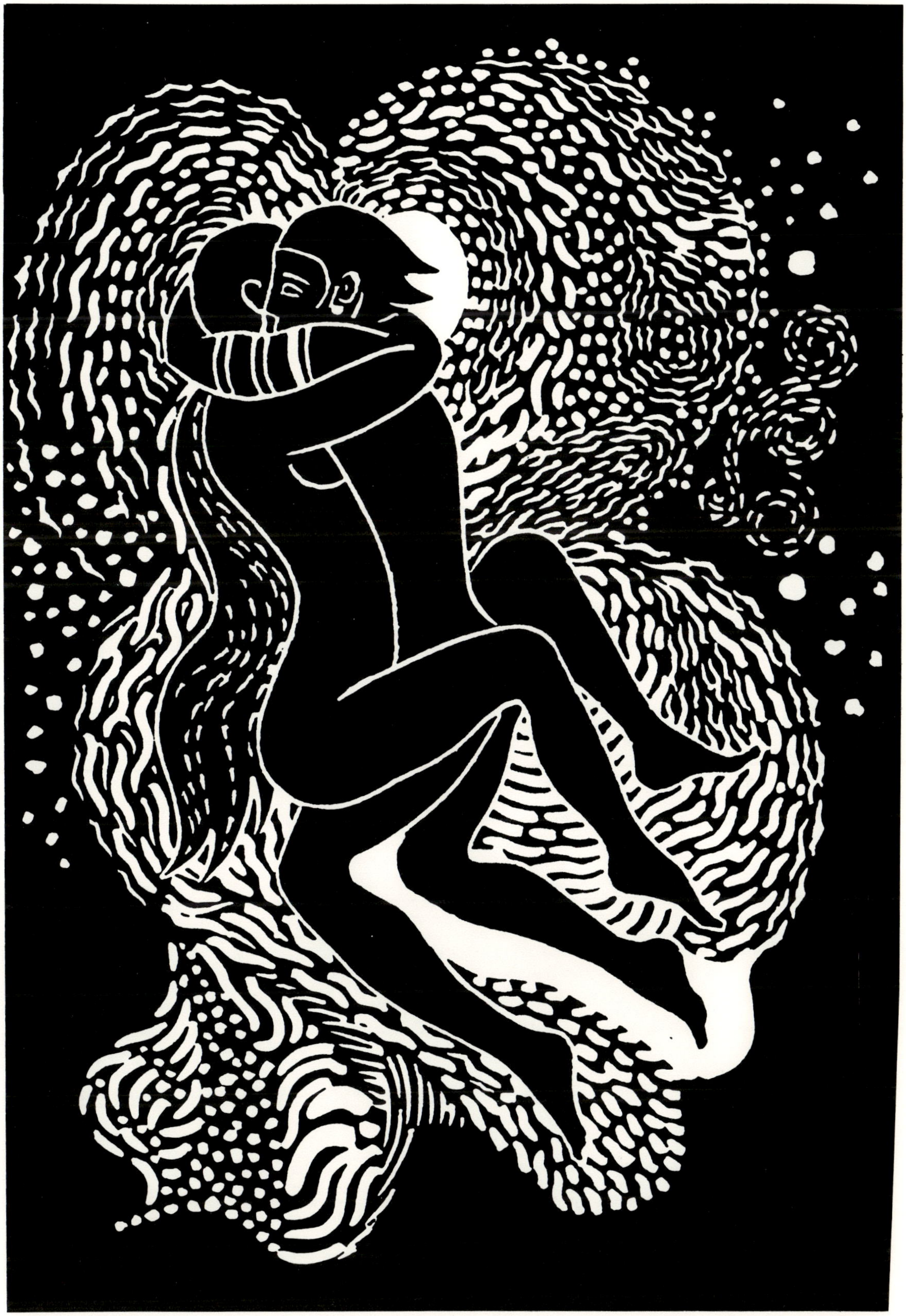

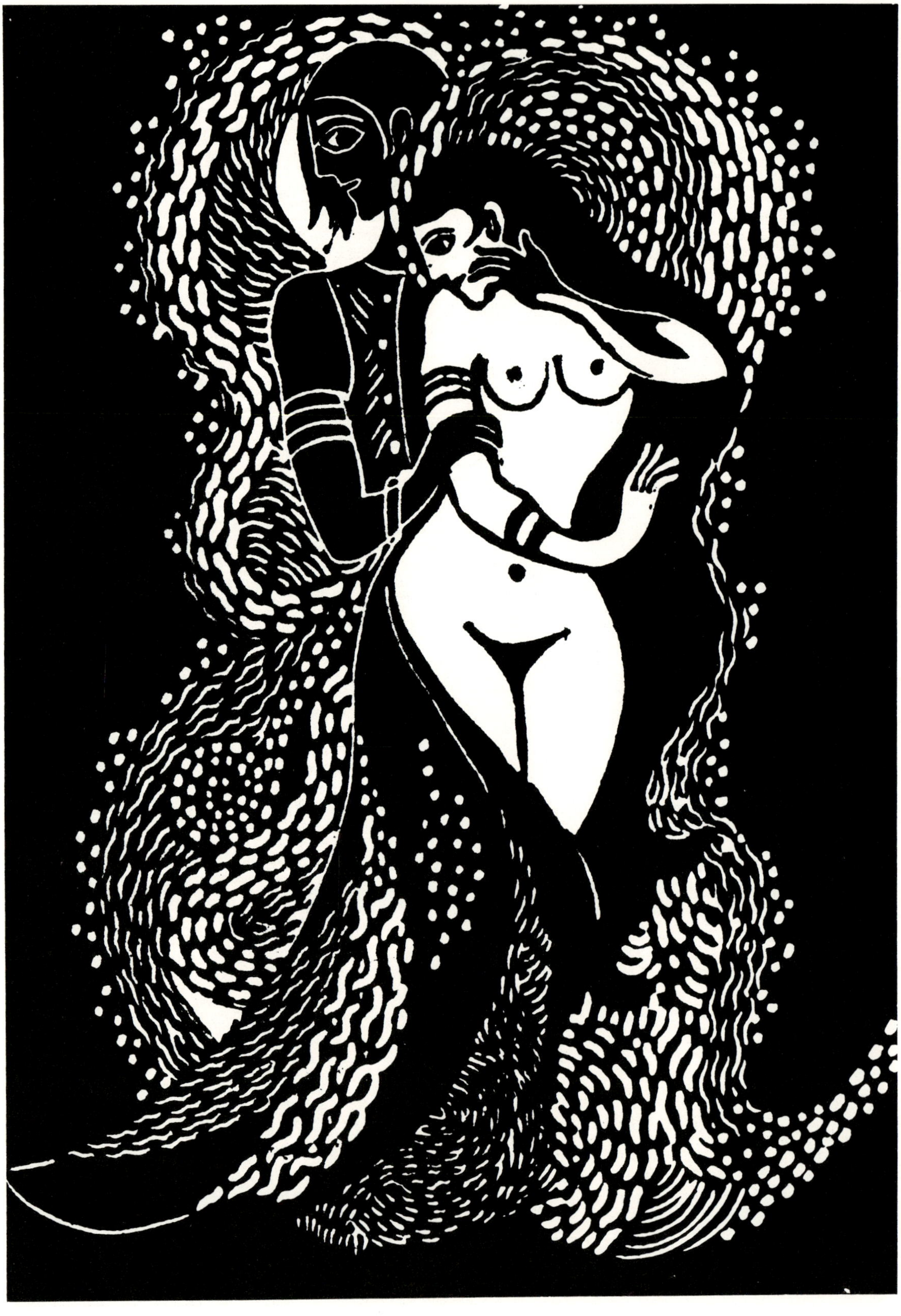

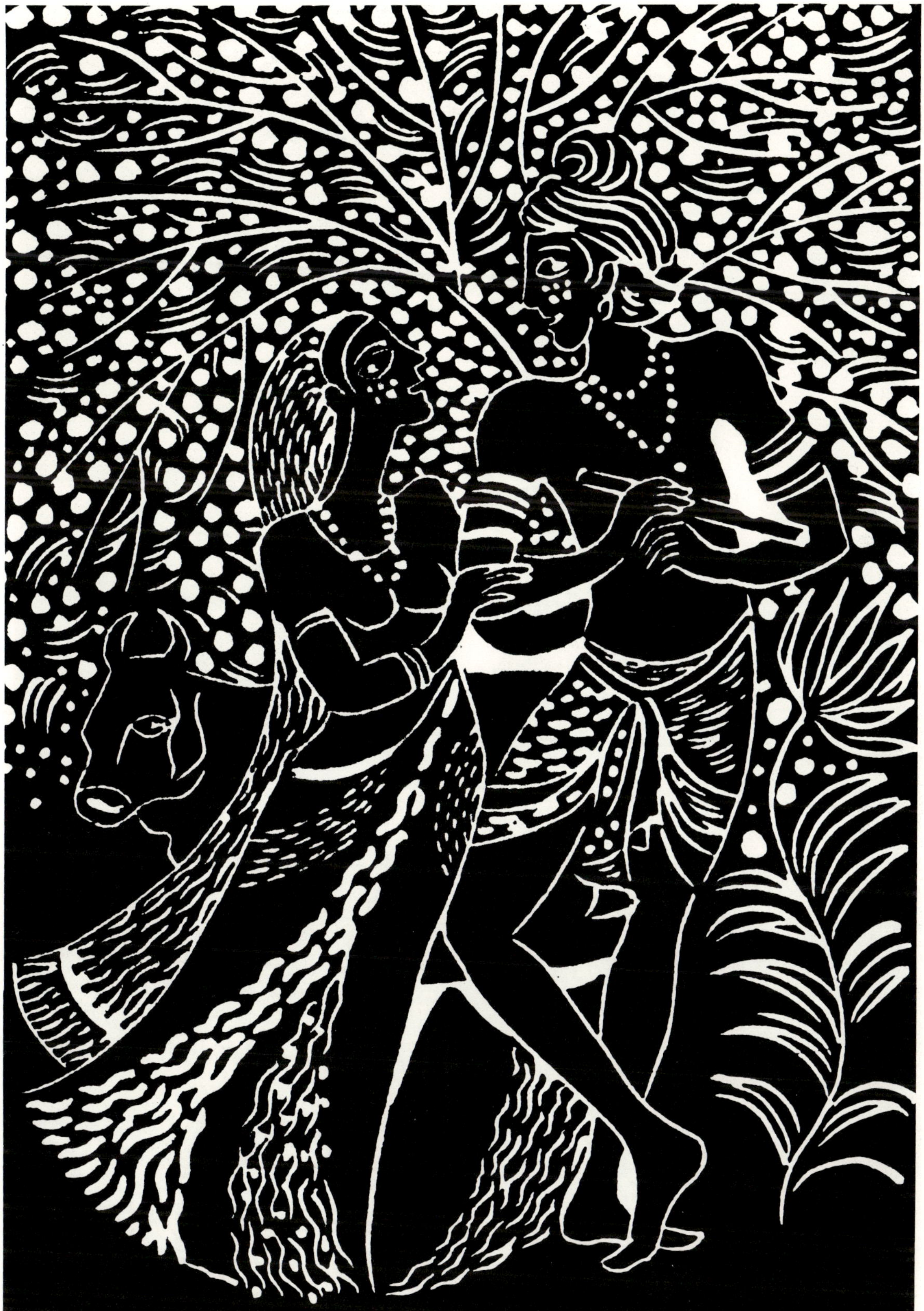

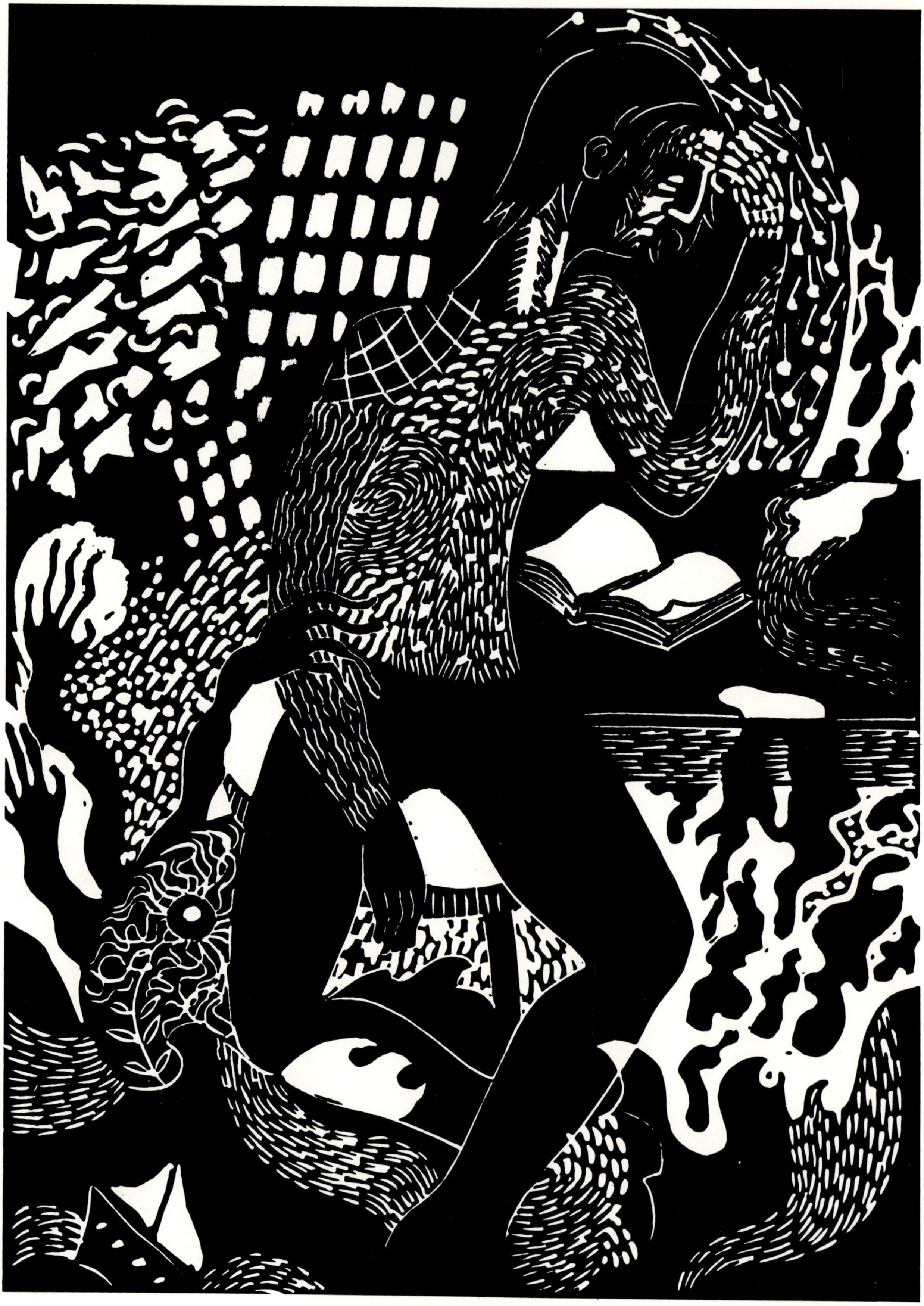

Cast out

Remember that

Any being

Is all being,

From the beginning

That never began,

To the end

That will never end.

Remember that...

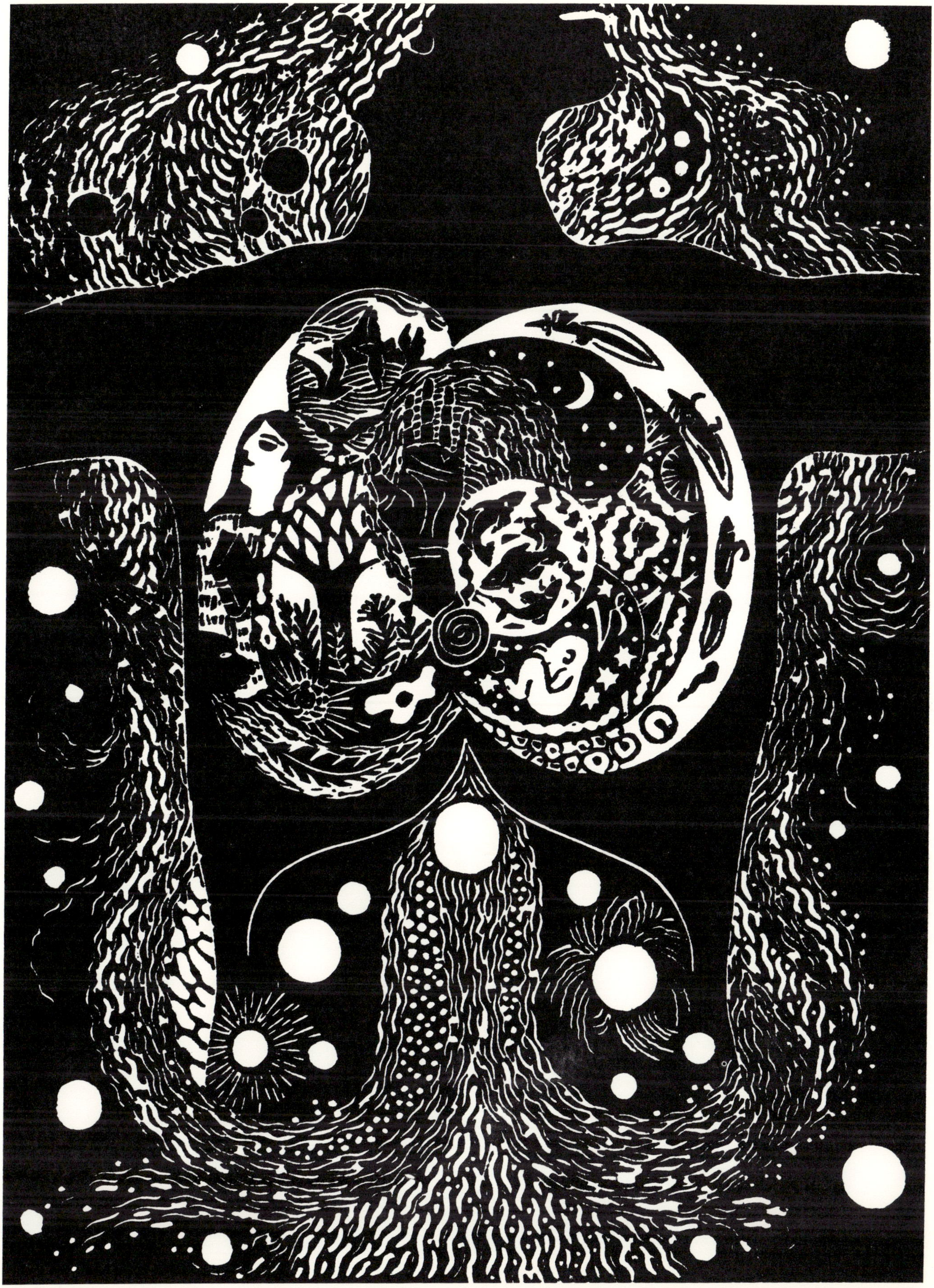

For years uncounted

The sequoia grows

Unbent

By fire, foe, and storm,

Until his death

In silence.

Man thirsting for life

Blooms in strength

With brilliant thoughts

And deeds

And dominates the world.

Fate comes suddenly

Unannounced,

Cancer, War,

Insanity, Despair.

The heavens remain silent

And we

Cry.

Dying

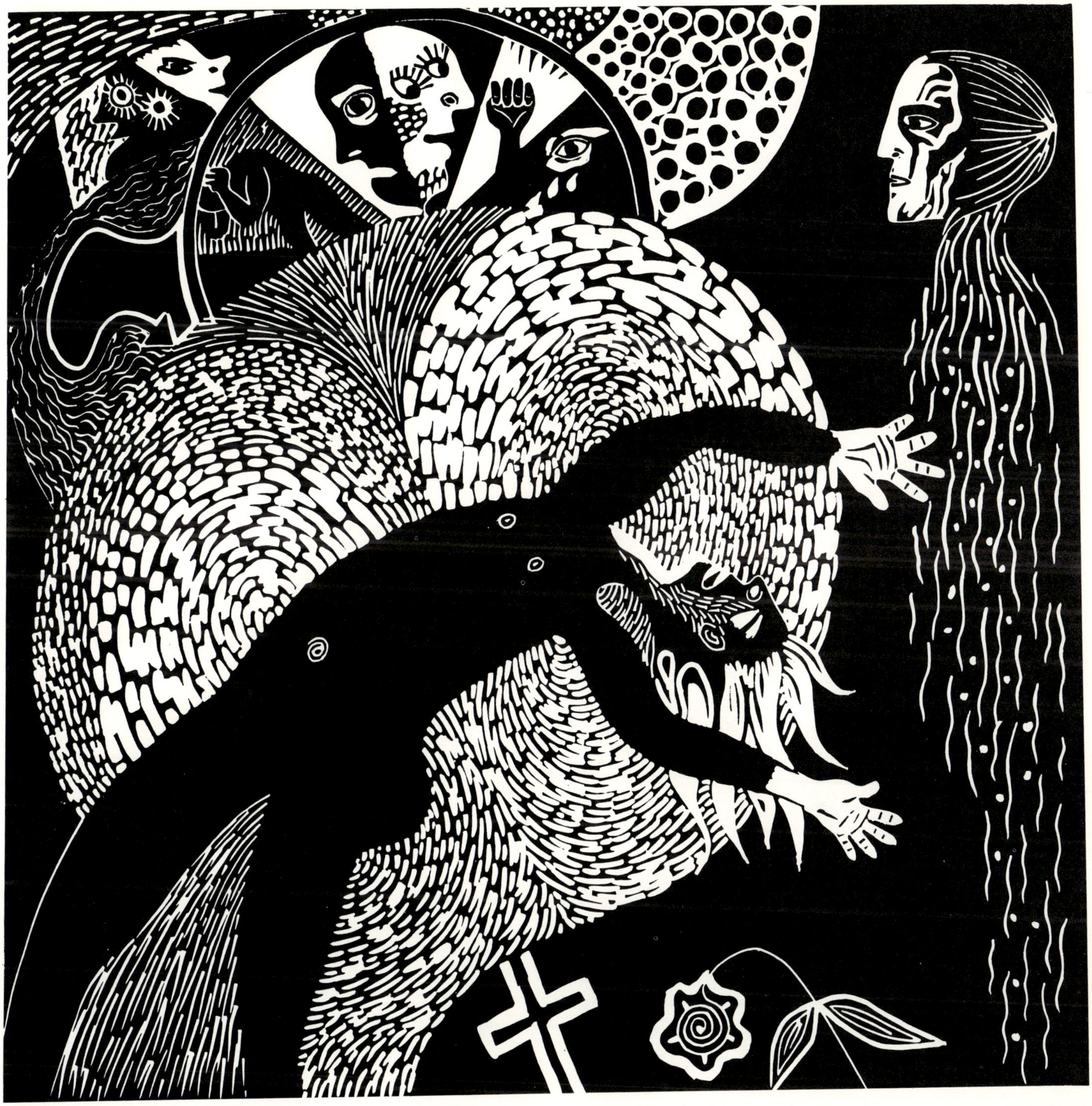

Man builds bridges,

Aeroplanes and ships,

Gives food and shelter,

Medicine,

For millions longer life---

And death to others.

He has no time

To love and laugh,

Or see

A child in need,

To marvel

At the butterfly,

The eagle,

Man,

Has no place to go.

T

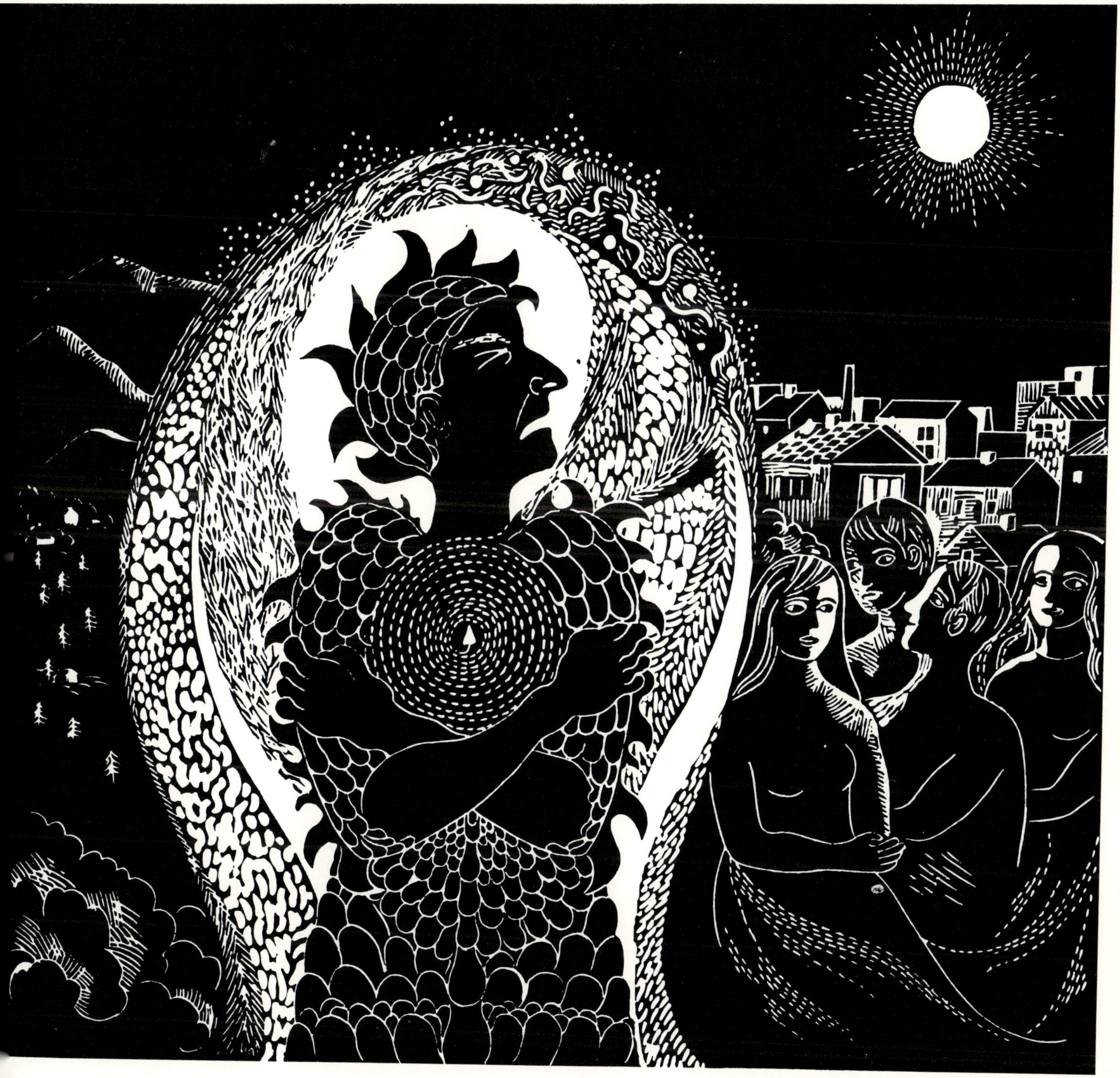

Uninvited

Enters the cold night,

Penetrates and chills

Your heart,

Strikes biting blows

To wound and kill.

Darkness

Creeps into your blood,

Your mind is hazy

And your touch is cold.

Your thoughts are daggers

Invisible

Weapons against trees and flowers

Animals and friends,

The bearing ground

Of your life.

Self destruction

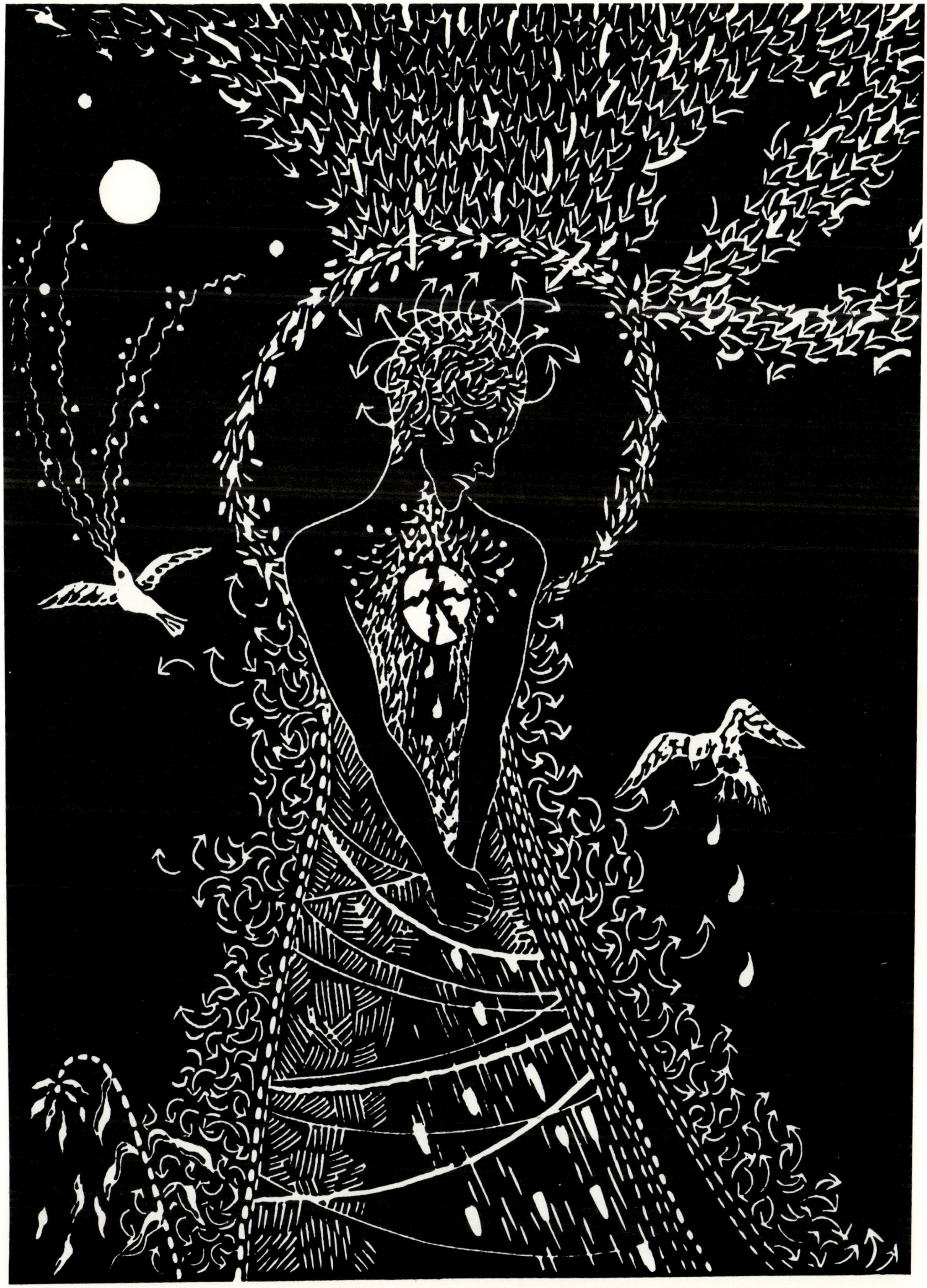

Deadly is

The evil in your heart

And "knowledge"

Of God.

Corrupt as

Pleasure, pain

The ever-lurking foe

Of man.

Luring us

To join his

Certainty and power

To dominate and rule.

But freedom,

The holy flower,

Still grows

In the desert.

Watered

By the tears

Of a thirsting

Wanderer.

Evil

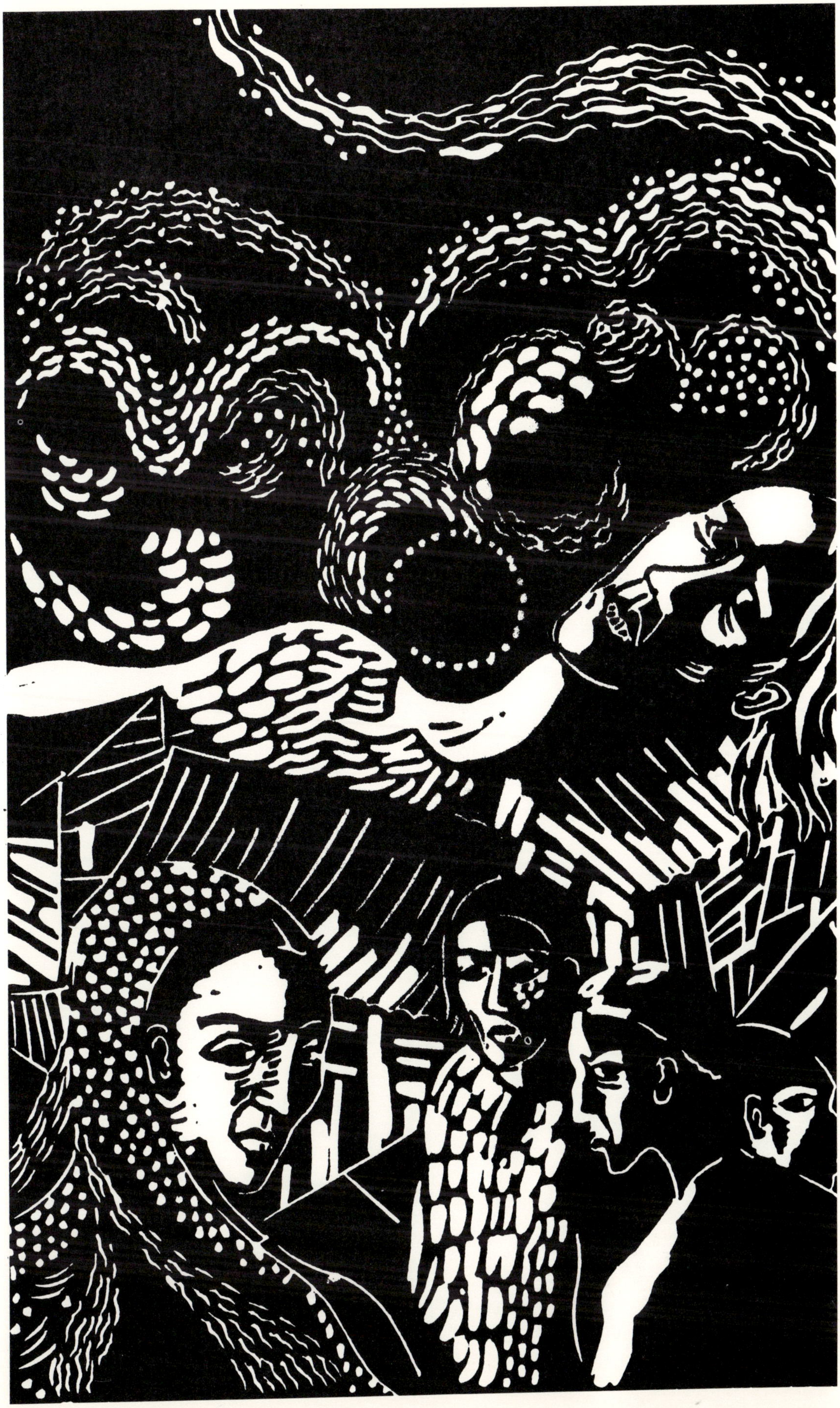

In weary times

Of ignorance

And bleeding rivers,

Of screaming Earth

And weeping Sky,

When flowers die

And trees of careless hands,

When mountains shiver in despair---

    Be still

    And listen.

Hibernation

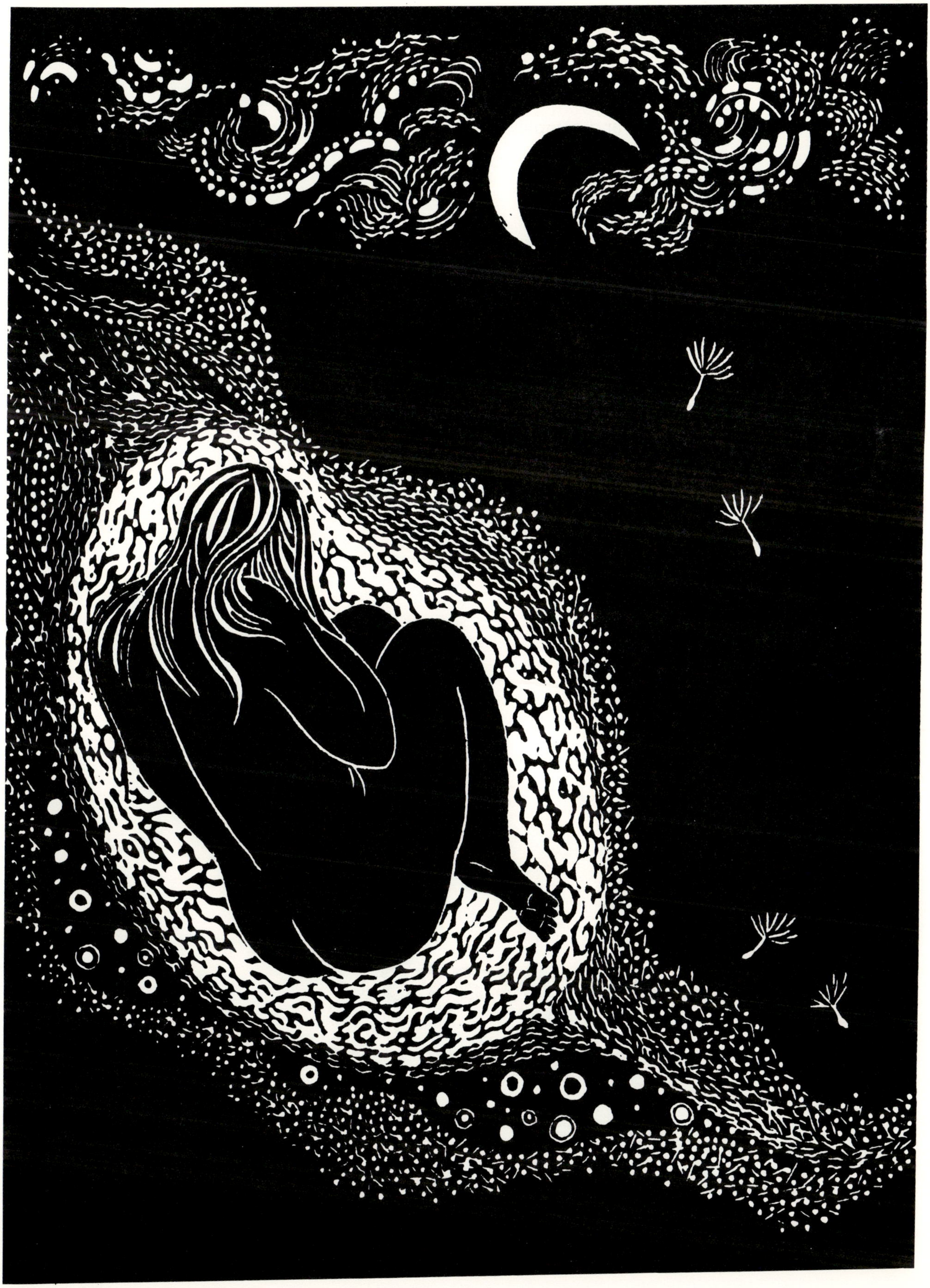

Man prays

In churches and temples

To his hopes and fears;

Forgotten

The unknown God.

But in the ocean

The dolphin sings,

And in mountain peaks

The eagle.

And a woman

And a man

Is free—

    To listen.

Man prays

With longing branches

Deeply rooted in the

Waters of the Earth

Stands the Oak.

Receiving light

From sun and stars,

Exhaling life

Through tender leaves,

And resting mightiful

Within the Ground.

Alive through ages

Watching busy men

In war and fight,

Giving gifts of shadow,

Rest and peace,

Sharing secrets with

The wise of silent,

Bending, moving, strength.

And under his majestic crown

Protecting

The tenderness of the blue flower.

The Oak

The Old Ones
Never die
Nor did they ever live,
    They are
In oldest tales
Of Gods walking on earth,
In cities
Timeless resting
At a river's bend,
Or high on mesas
Harbors of the seas.
    They are
In poets singers,
Women and the wise,
The unmoved mover
Of the wind
And man's affairs,
The spirit
Breathing life of a new time
Into a fresh mind.
    They are
Present—timeless—
In man, his love and sorrow,
Caring for a child,
The trusting eyes
Of animals
Innocent in need and plea.
    They are.

SONG:

  The Heaven
Bears the Waters
    Bears the Ground
The Grounding
    Of the Waters
        Of the Heaven

The Spirit
Bears the Mind
    Bears Thoughts
The Thinking
    Of the Mind
        Of the Spirit

Tree of Life

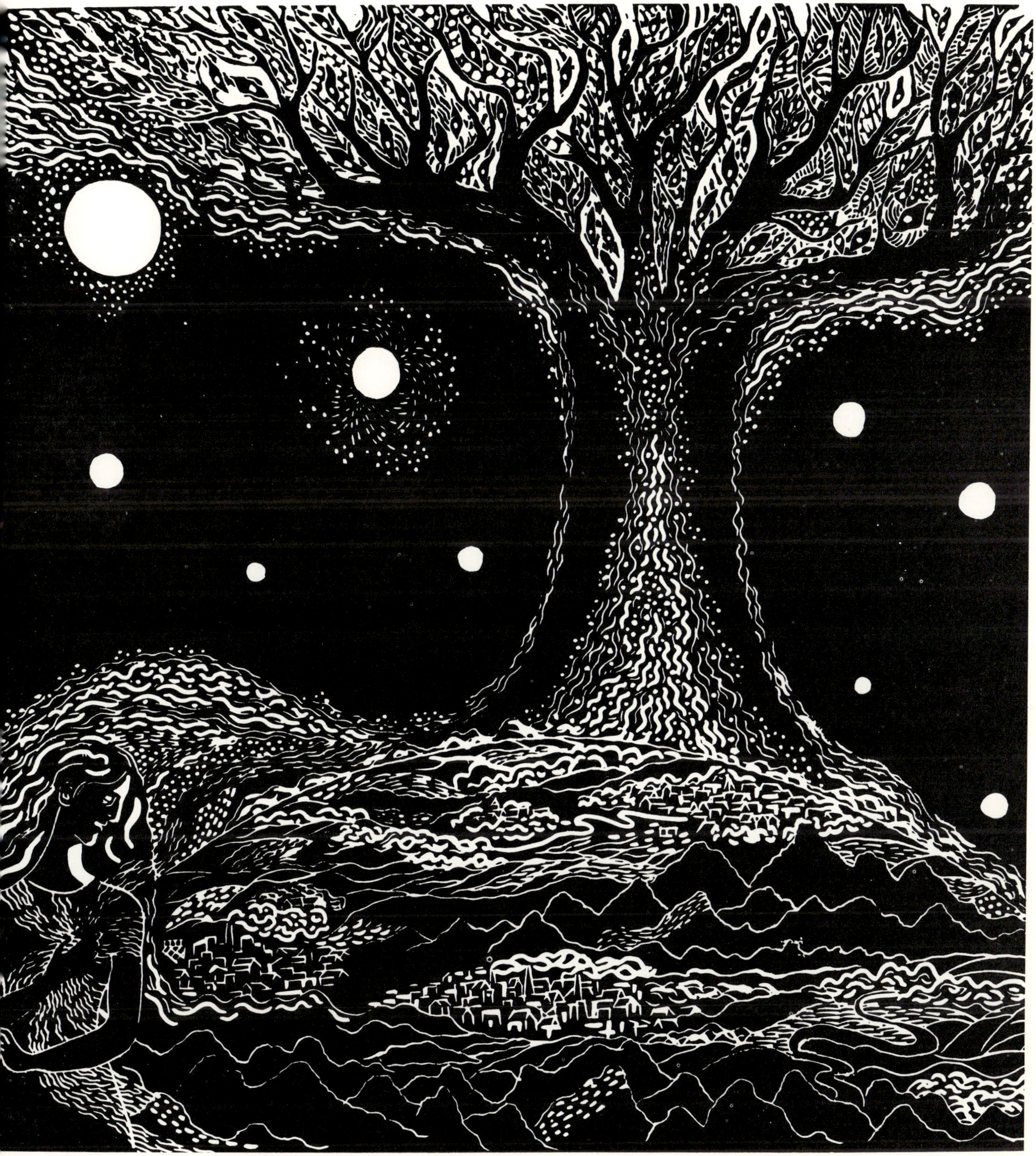

LOGICAL THOUGHT

IS LIKE A TOWER

SOLID, RIGID,

COLD AND STRONG.

Within a floating, waving valley,

    Green with joyful grass and full

        of living, rivers, trees, and flowers.

Thoughtwebs

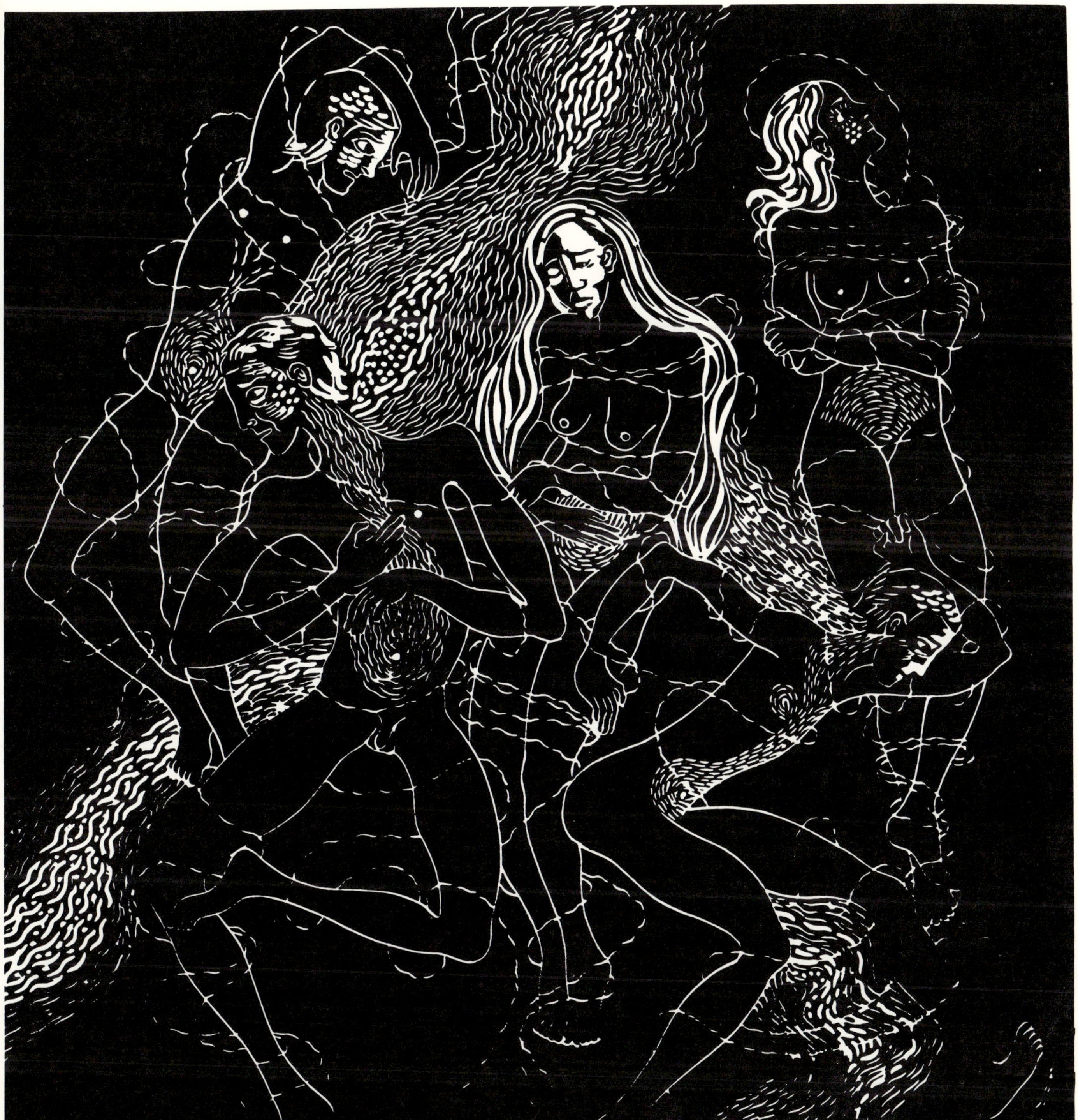

Where is love

When people scream

In agony, starvation

Of food

Or a mere friendly hand,

When hatred flares

To kill in lust

And in despair,

When life is vaporized

In an atomic blast?

Where is mystery

When animals

Alive with oldest eyes

Of suffering and wisdom

Without words

Are slaughtered,

Bred to death

In millions,

To tickle a palate?

Driven

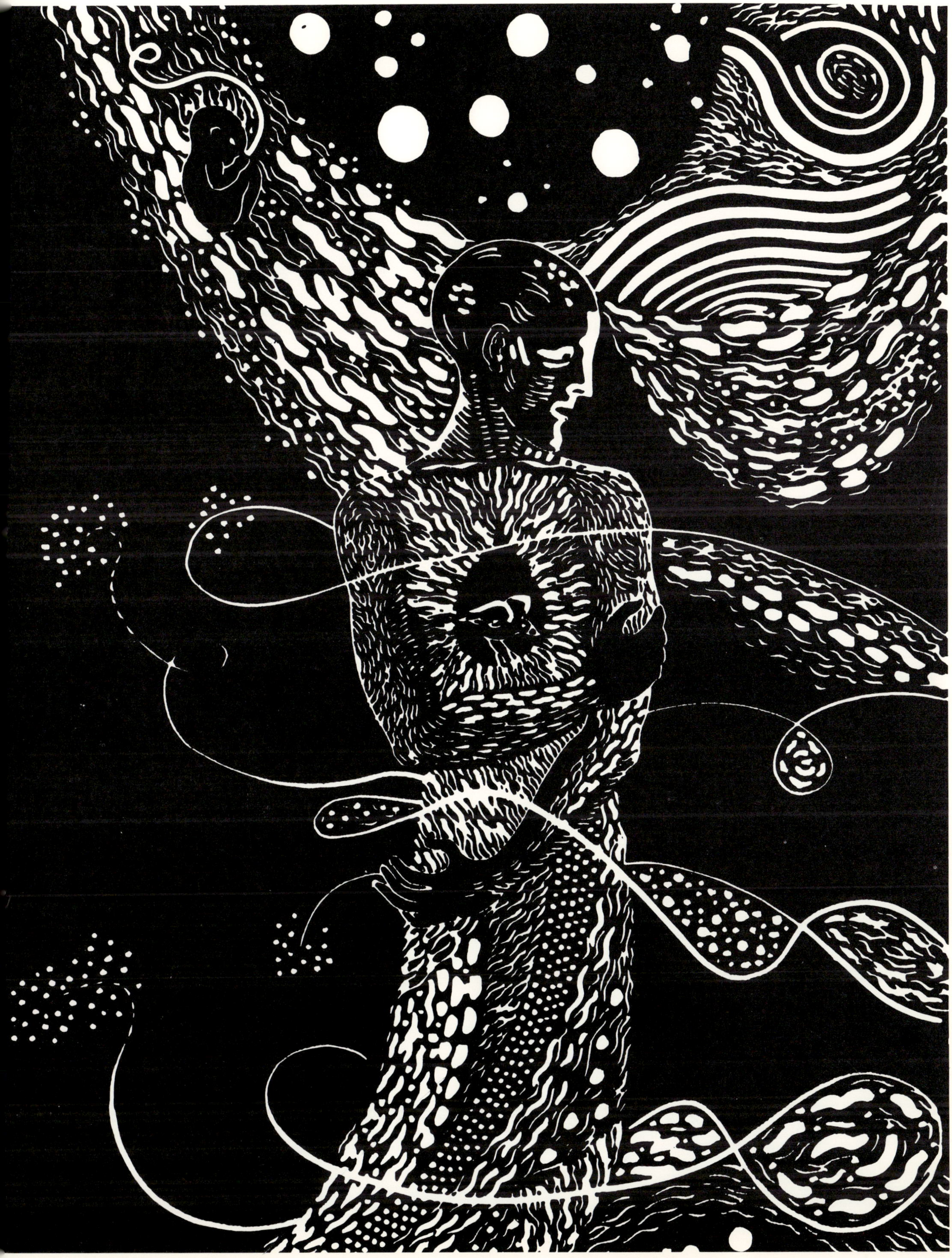

WANDERER'S NIGHTSONG

Silence is

Over the forest's leaves.

In the branches

You hardly sense their breath.

The birds are quiet

In the greening hill,

Just wait,

So soon,

You also---will be---

Still.

                Goethe

Stillness

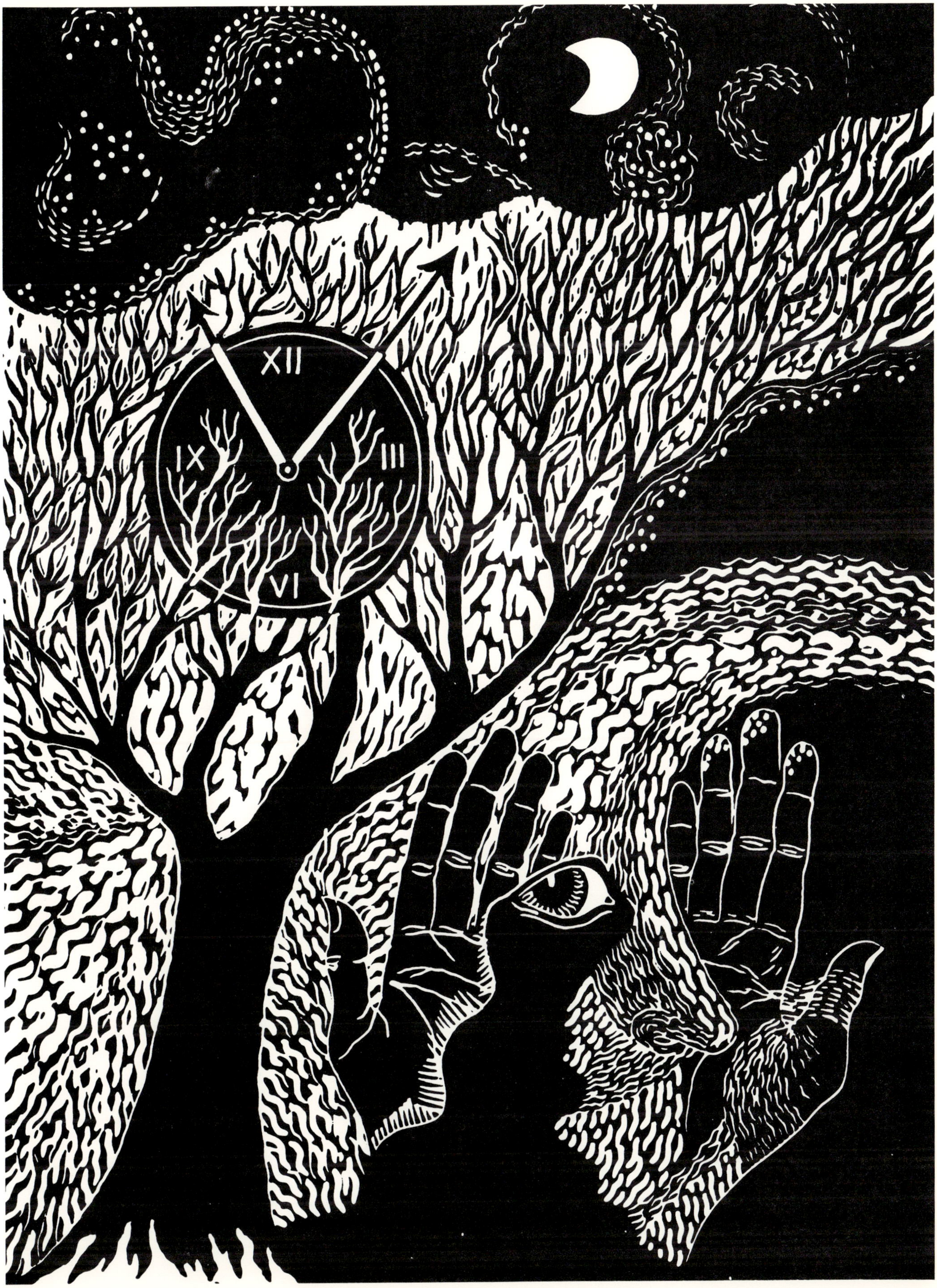
XII
IX
III
VI

The self

With

Mind and body?

The self

    Of

        Mind

           Of

              Body

    Moving

Mind

    Of

        Self

           Of

              Body

    Moving

Body

    Of

        Mind

           Of

              Self

    Moving

Bound and free

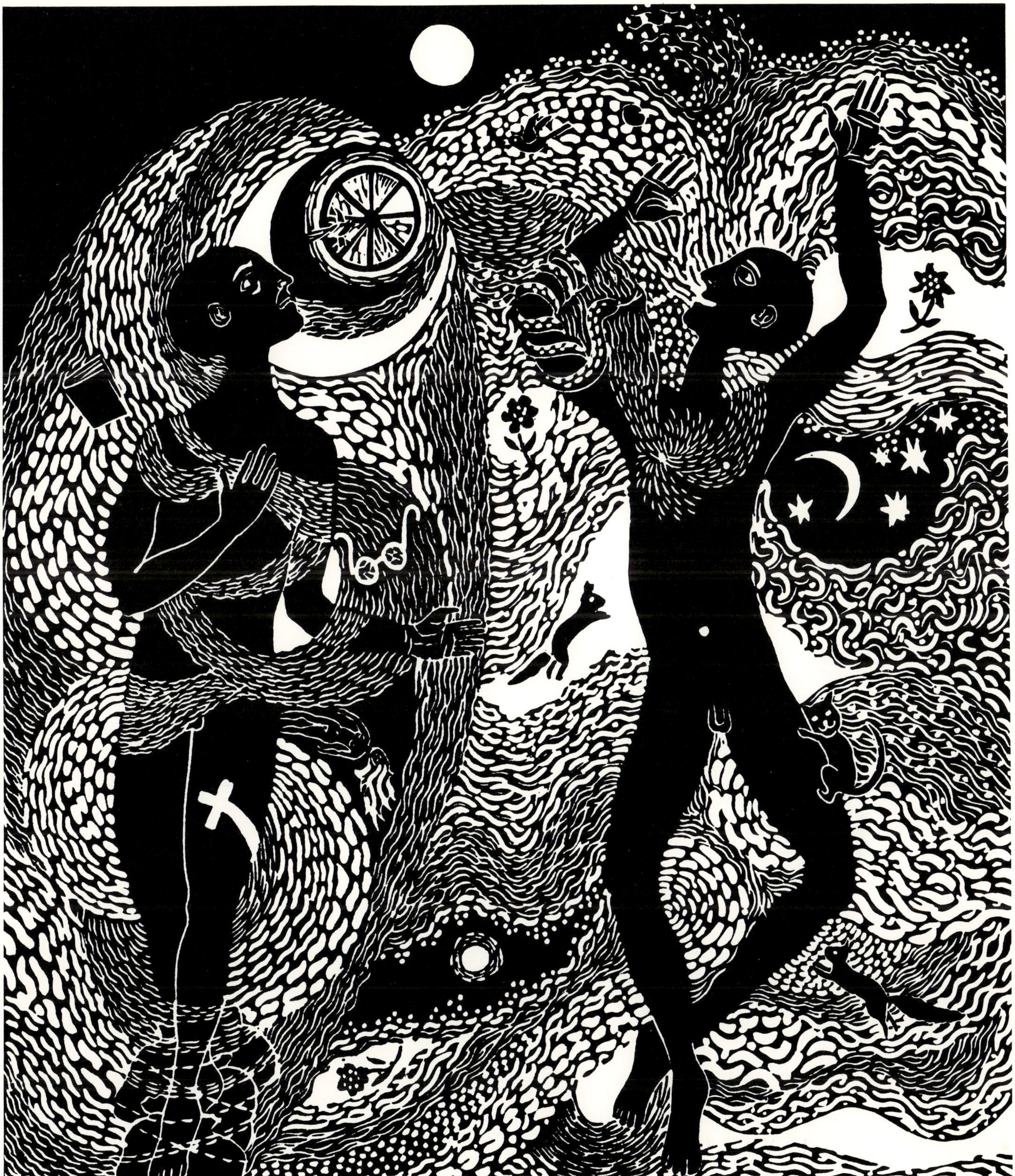

Man,

    Shaper of the earth,

       Conquerer of planets,

Knows not

       Himself.

Imprisoned

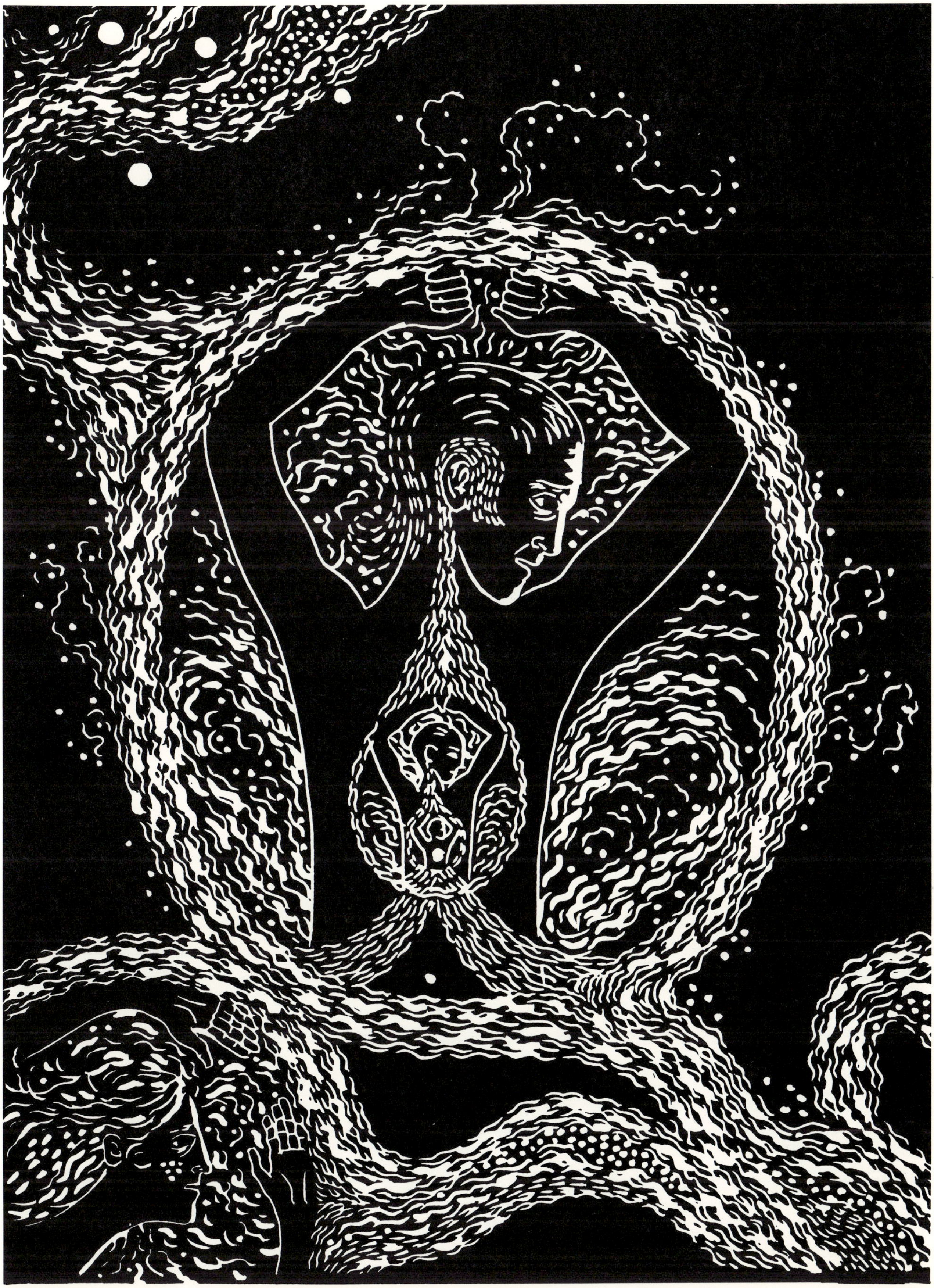

Freedom

    Most precious

    Gem of Gods,

    Sought

    Through oceans full

    With screaming blood,

    Sold by priests

    And eye-less saints,

    Promised by the prophets

    Of happiness

Is in man.

Free

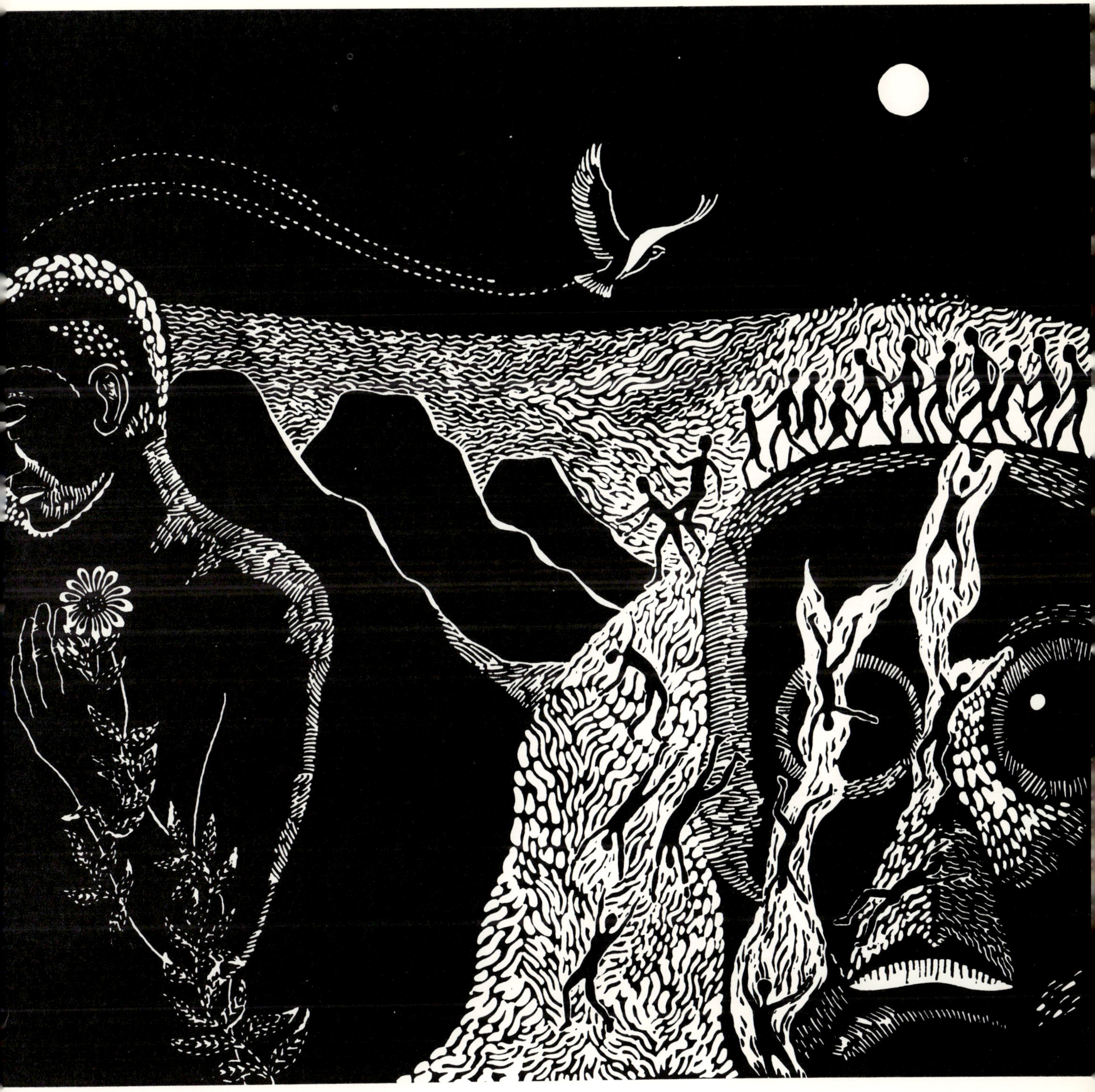

Not anymore

Are you a stranger to yourself.

Already joy is there,

And whispering of unknown life.

Look through the shadows

To the light they veil.

Receive the Muses' gifts

And let them guide you

Past steep gorges

Of rigid rights.

To the waters.

Floating,

Between the mysteries

Of Earth and Sky

Next step

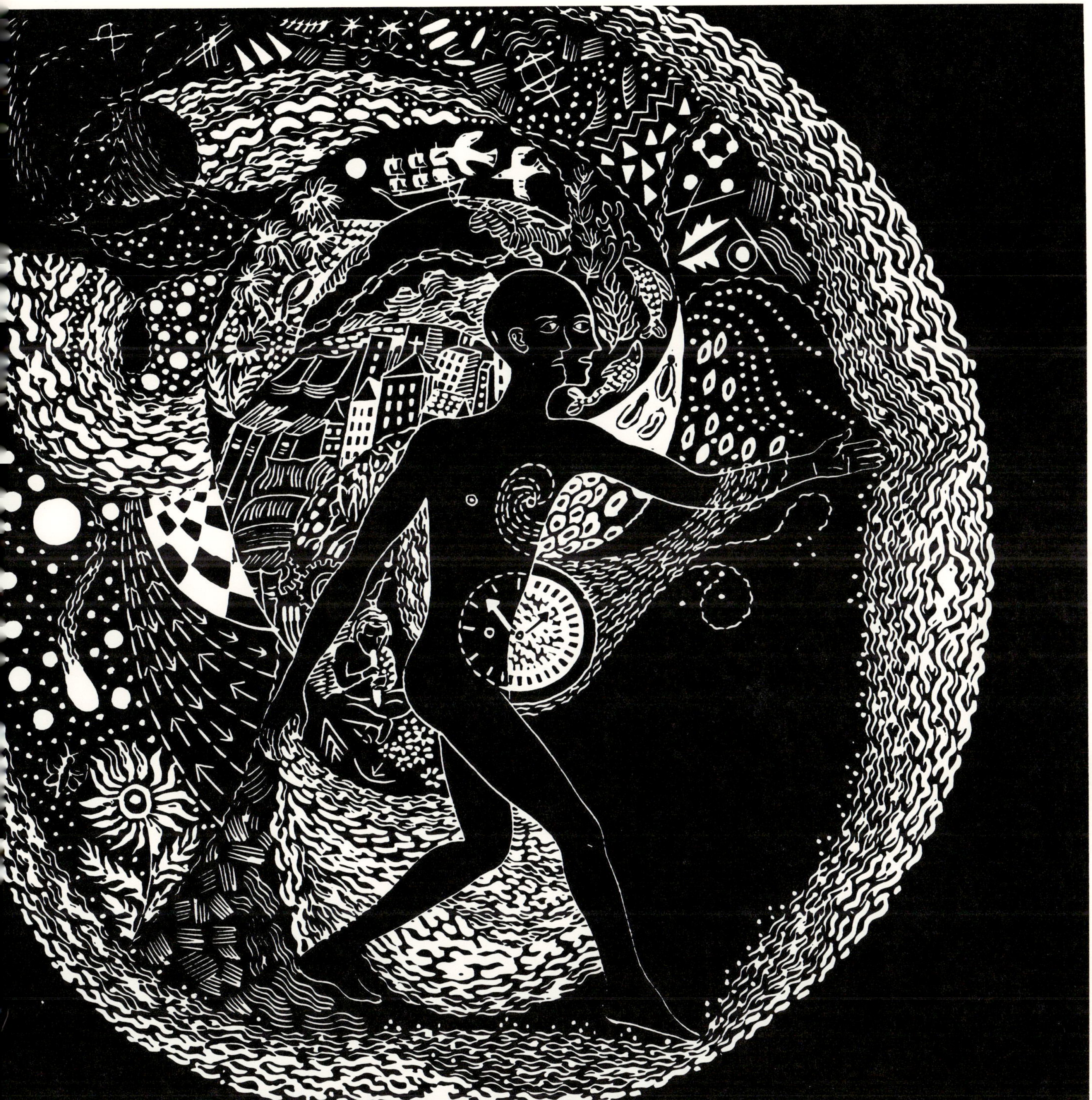

Be brave and build!
Strong Heart and healthy hands
The cathedral of tomorrow
Of a new mind.

Cut with a sharp knife
Of knowledge and of faith
The cobwebs of the past,
Illusions and deceits,
Bound by time,
To open wide your heart
For love's creative tune,
Of lonesome tears
Sparkling in the thousand colors
Of a new life.

Look in the raindrops of
The mirror formed by
Brittle autumn leaves
To see the rules unruled,
The everchanging
Rhythmic dance
Of a dreaming universe.

Be brave

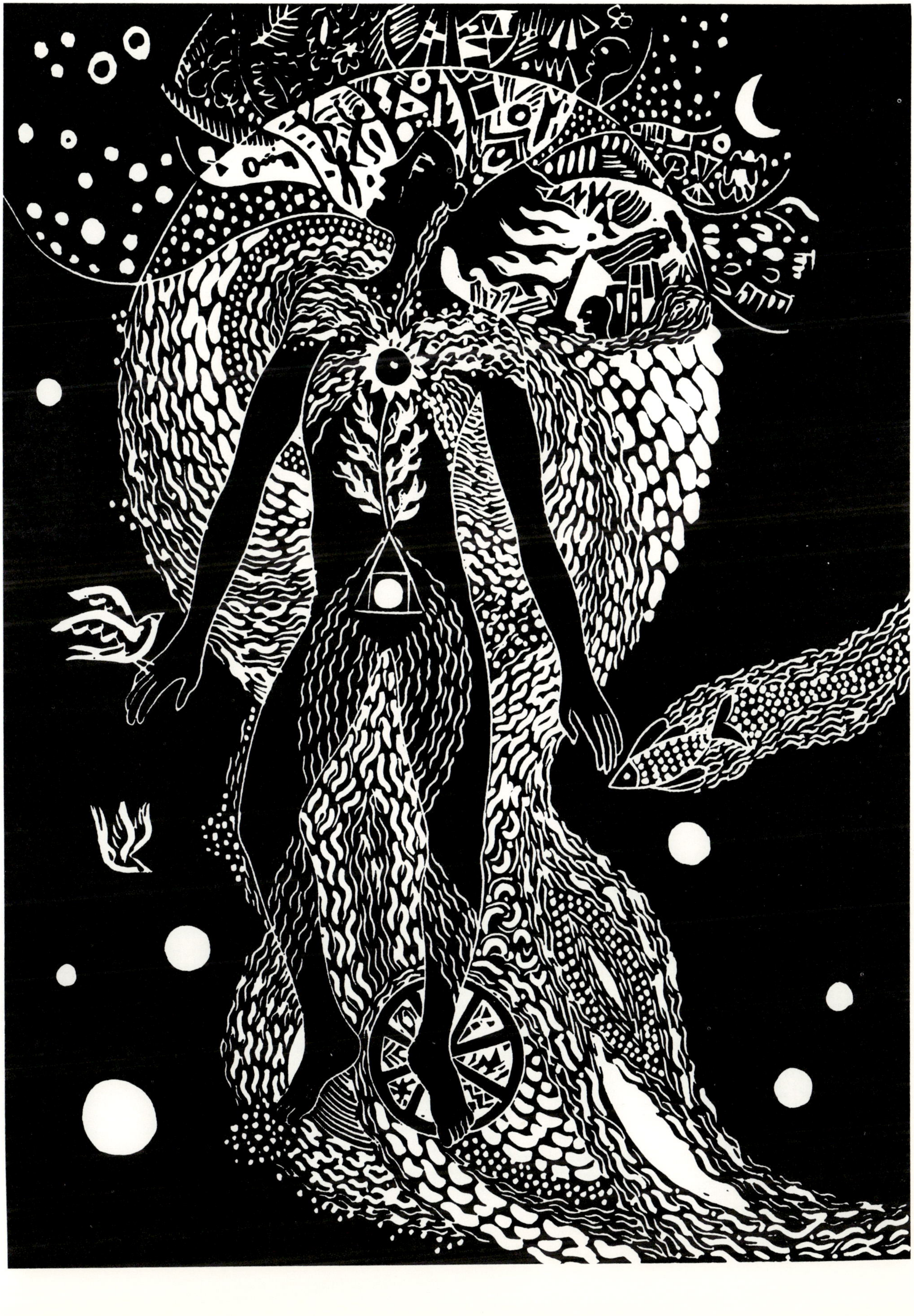

Human is
A fighting man
Who knows himself
Man and woman,
A mother's child,
Suffering
With wife and friends,
Hoping and afraid,
Of himself,
Of another
Fighting man.

Human is
A fighting man
Who sees
The misery,
Broken branches
Of a wasted land,
Waters fouled
And air,
Himself,
The hope of
Other fighting men.

Human is
A fighting man
Who loves,
Respects the other's cause,
Who knows
That truth is not
In any book
Nor thought nor sword,
But may be
For moments
Like light reflecting
In the morning's dew
In the struggle
With another
Fighting man.

Warrior

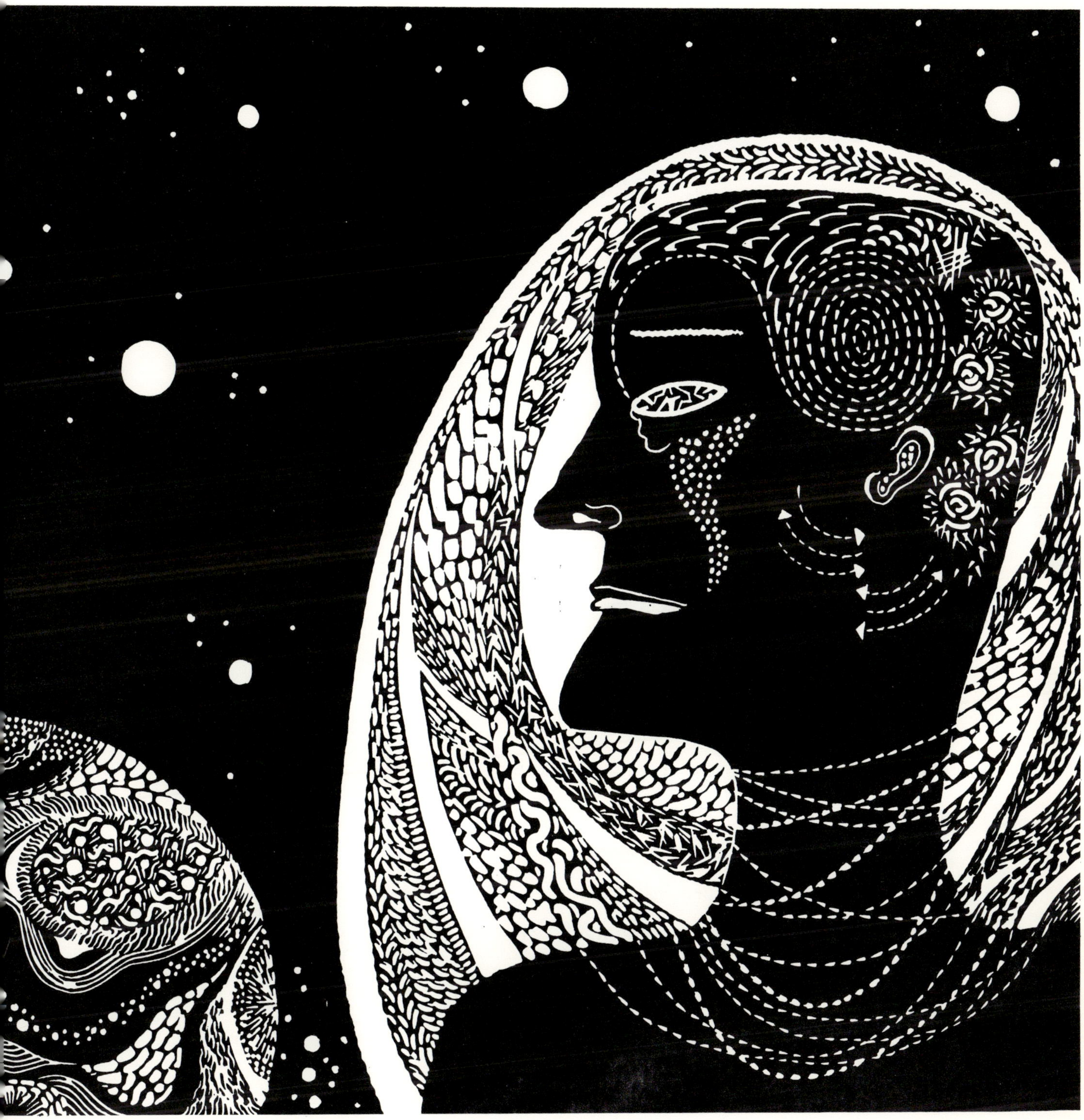

There is a way,

The way that opens

When you take a step

And closes right behind,

The way that can't be seen

Or made up in the mind.

There one moves

Like birds a-flying

Through silver clouds

Of thoughtless thoughts,

There one's life is always dying

And ideas are joyous noughts.

There you're floating

Through a sea of flowers

Cradled by the golden sun,

Breathless breathing

Happy showers

Of everending

Timeless fun.

A way

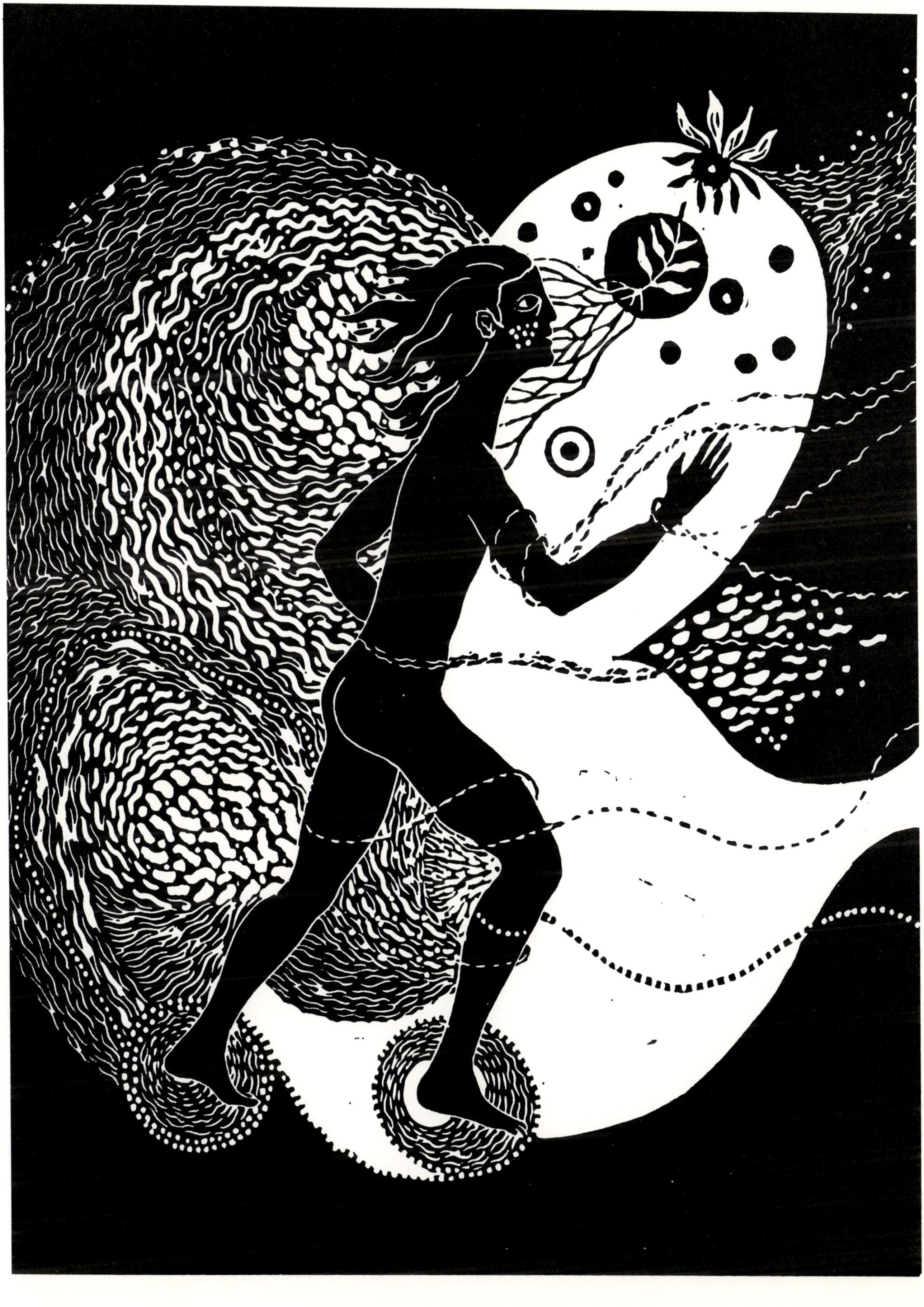

You can never step in the same river twice.

You are never the same to step in a river.

The same thought is never the same.

You, thought, the river,

Leaves in the autumn wind,

Colors of a rainbow,

Light, dancing in the dew.

Change

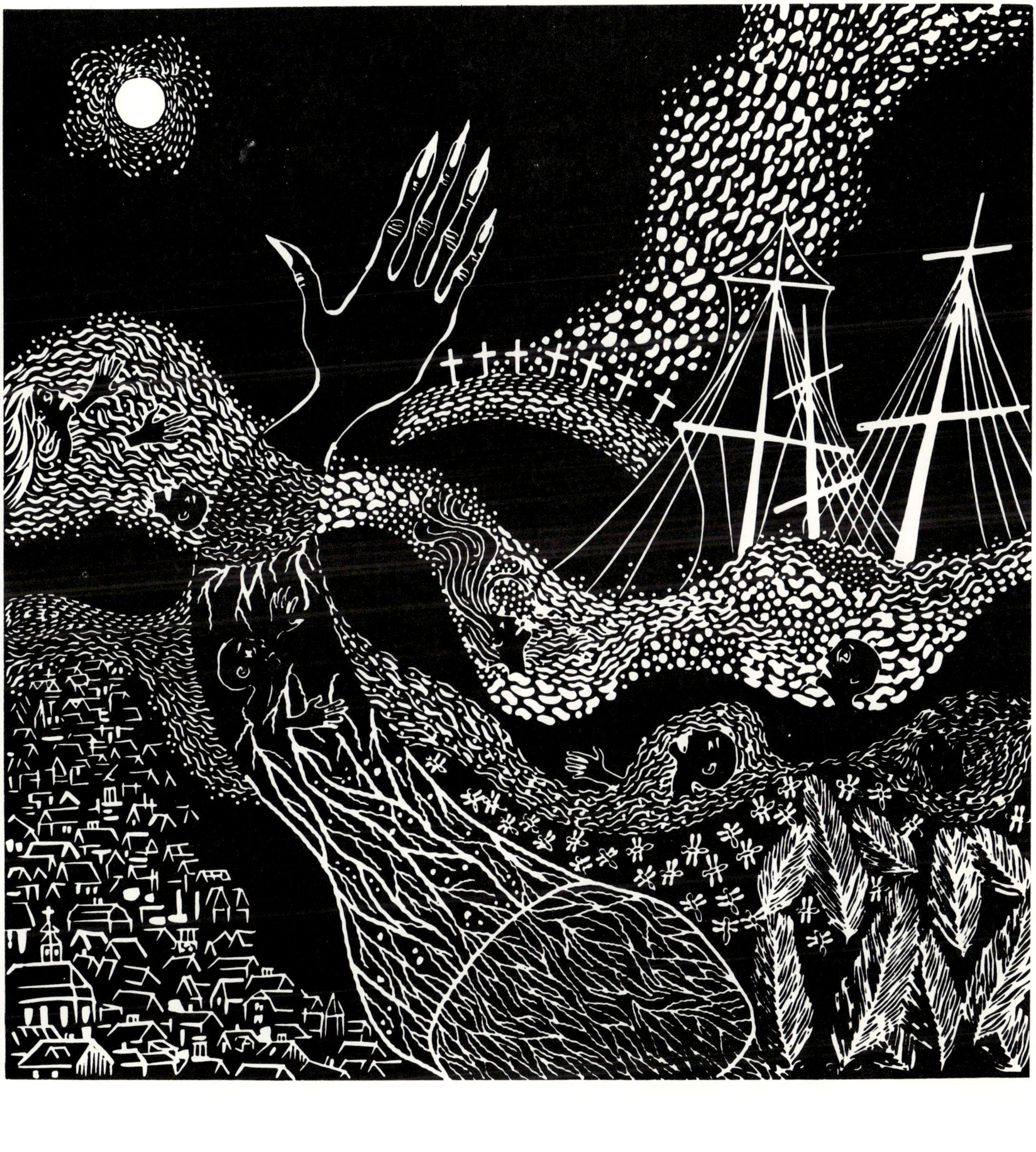

Honest, humble

With your own mistakes,

As friend

So live,

And love and build,

Of the eternal mind

And yet estranged,

As if abandoned

In a hostile cloud

Of knowing ignorance,

But floating, living

With a warming sun

And trees and waters,

Birds and beasts,

With mind and heart in

Deep embrace,

And free

To love and comprehend

The Mind of Man and

---All---.

Man on his way

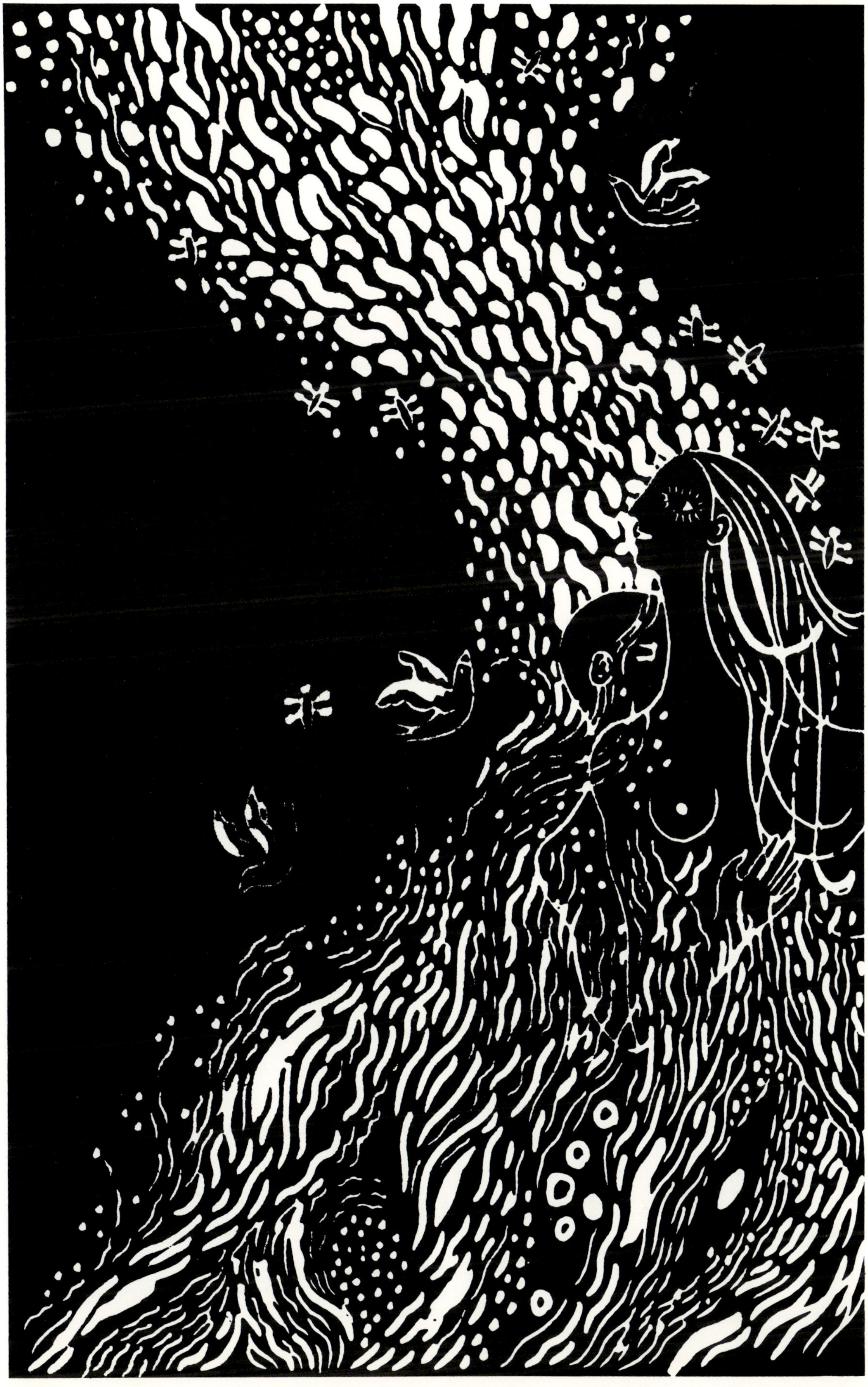

Man,

Alone

Knowing,

Rooted deep in time

Of wisdom and of

Freedom,

Of war and of

Oppressed humanity.

A seedling

Of the old forest,

Alone,

Struggling towards the sun;

But in the shadow,

Cast of aged and

Anxious leaves

Grows hope

For a

New time.

Seedling

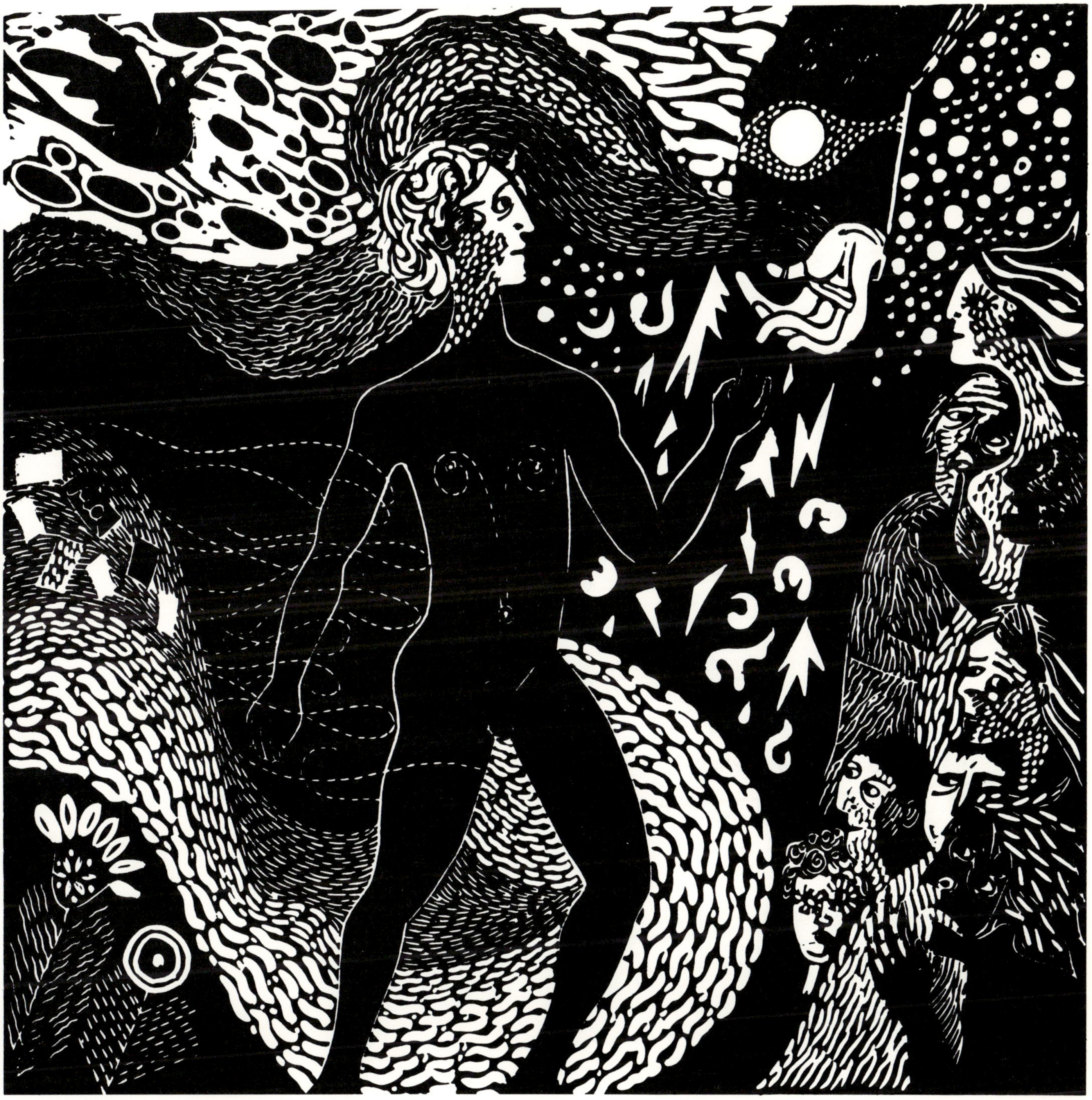

I saw the spirits play

In raging clouds of fear,

Embroidered by the ruling sun.

They waved their hands

Like to a caring friend.

Promised help and guidance.

I have faith—not hope—

Put down the heavy garment of

My past and future—time—

Flying with the first birds

In joyful fear,

Clothed in feathers

Like our friends.

Flying, living, dying

To the unknown

Harmony of life

And death and of

A human being

Rooted in the earth.

Bird with roots

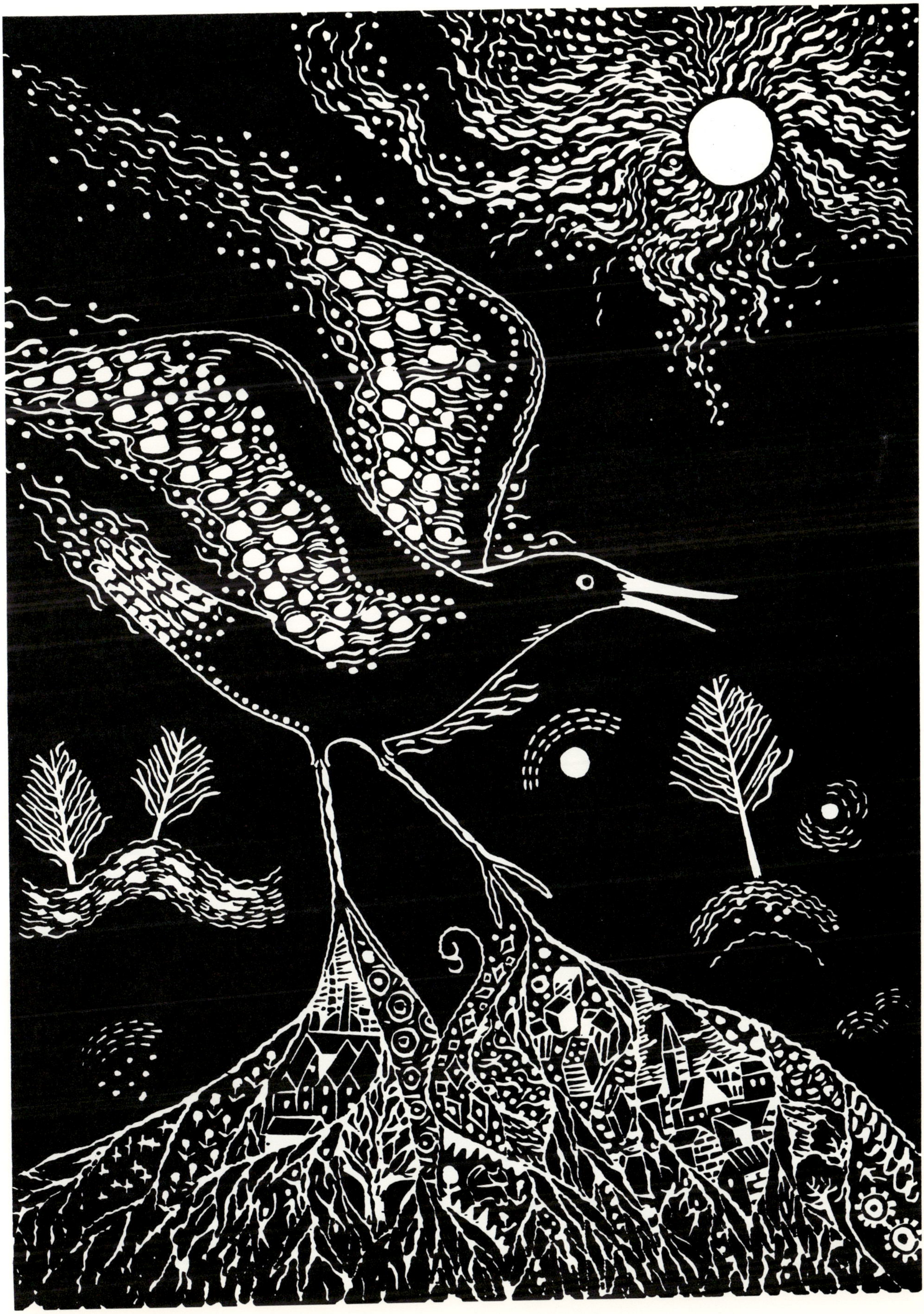

Wanderer!

You hesitate!

The mountain is so high!

And covered with eternal snow!

And your feet are tired!

You seek rest!

But in the highest ice

There blooms a flower

Blue and white,

Tender petals piercing

Through the freezing soil,

Warming your heart,

Calling on a friend

To visit her

In moonlit clouds

To share a moment

In love together,

To see the greening valley,

And,

To wander on.

Wanderer

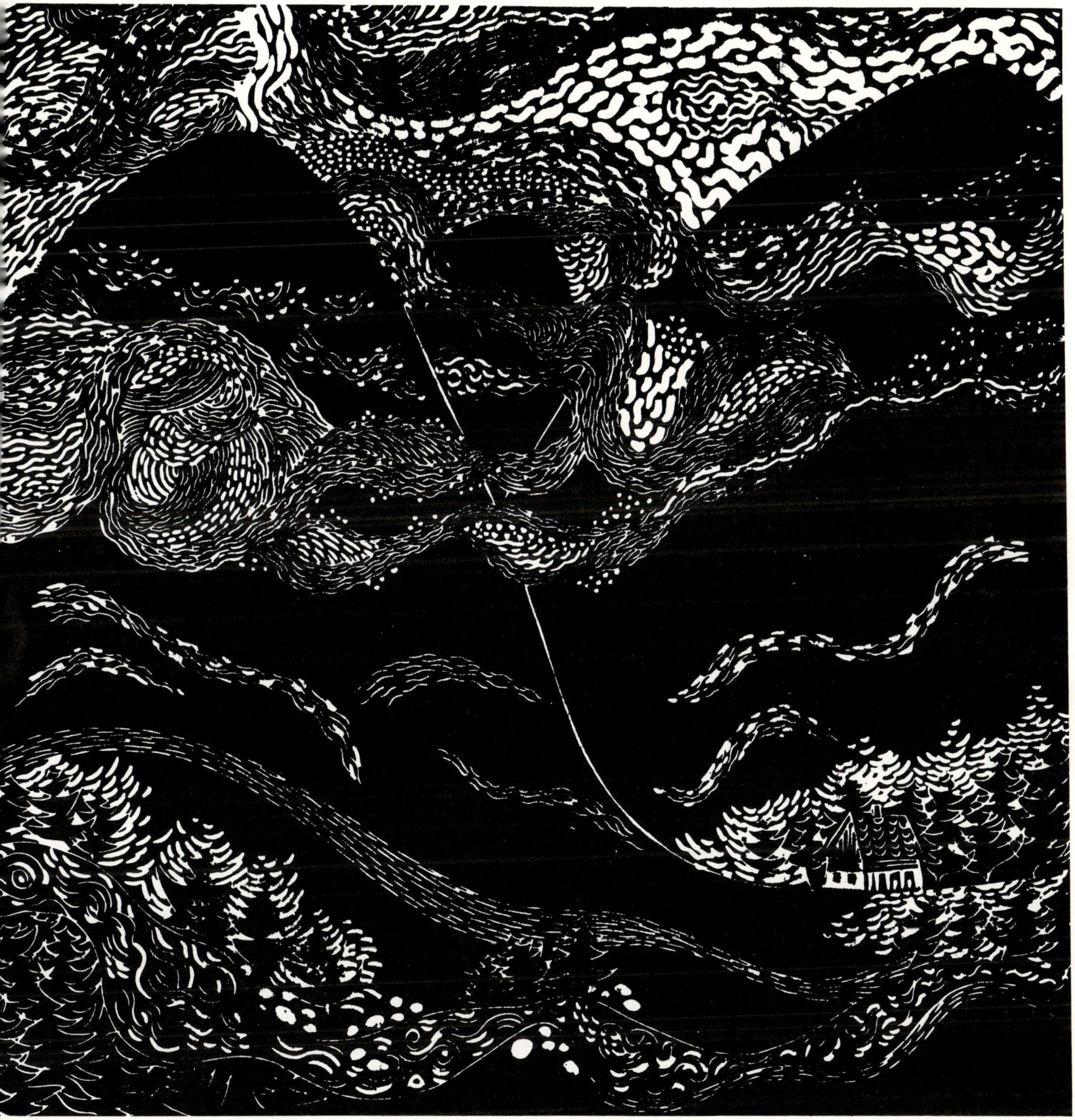

Bats whizzed in the cave,

The treetops swayed

Of darkness;

A star lit up

To stop

In a silent moment

The dance;

      And a man

      And a woman

      Looked up.

Dance

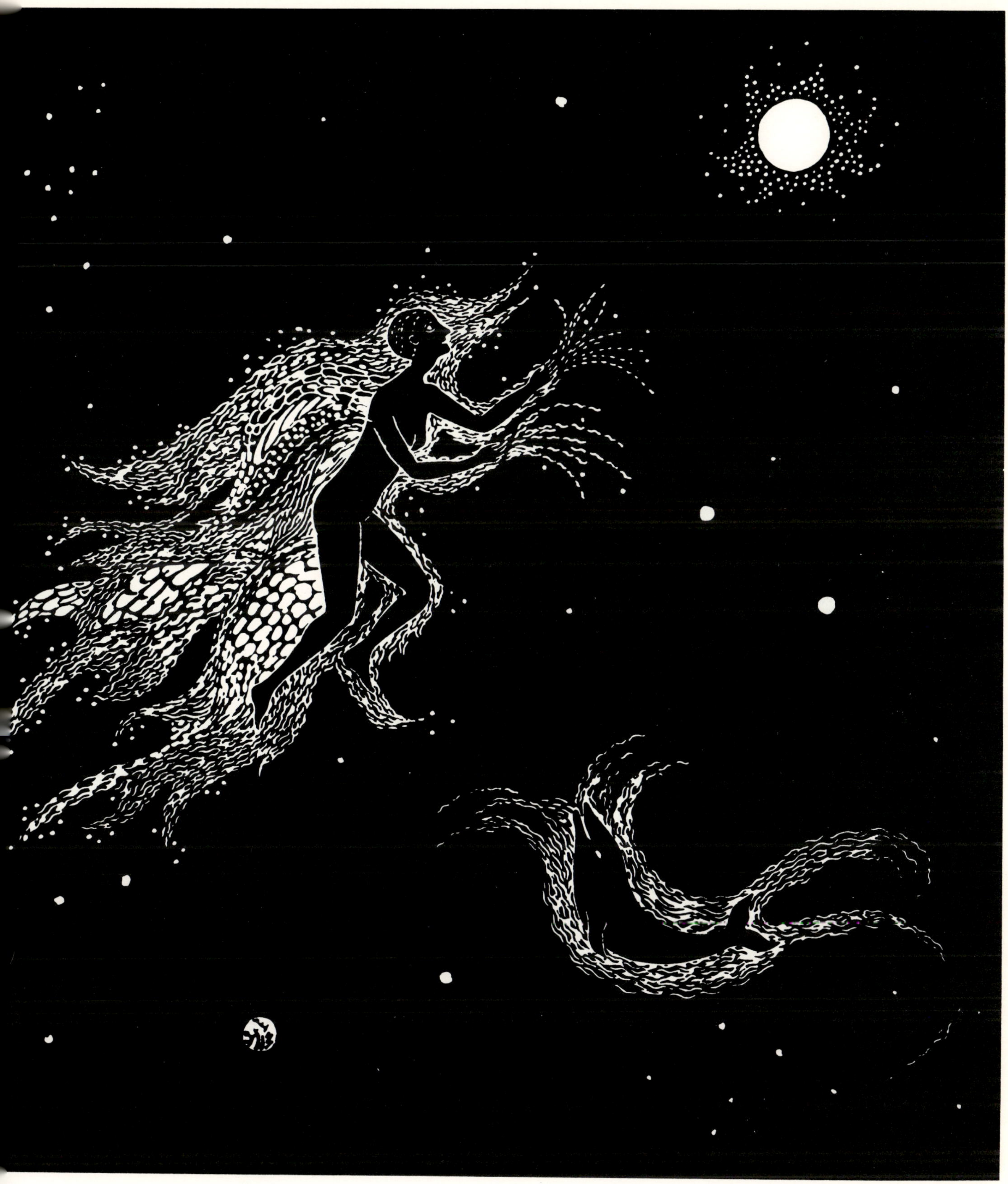

Mother of the Ground,
Source
Woman
Midwife
Styx.
Abused in slavery
Tied to home and bed
For a male's emptying whims,
Bound to follow and
Pursued as witch.

Preserving ancient wisdom.
Not knowing but
Sleepingly awake
Like the acorn
Waiting in a wedding soil.

Mother,
In the woman in the man,
Guardian of humanity,
Daring to join the devil,
To lure him,
Feel him
Deep inside
And to tie him
To his lust
And power.

Mother,
In the timeless tree,
Slumbering volcano,
Glowing emerald
And world beneath,
Your time has come!
To bring to life again
The dance,
To break the spell
Of our knowledge
Ignorance
Of a barren iron age.

Mother

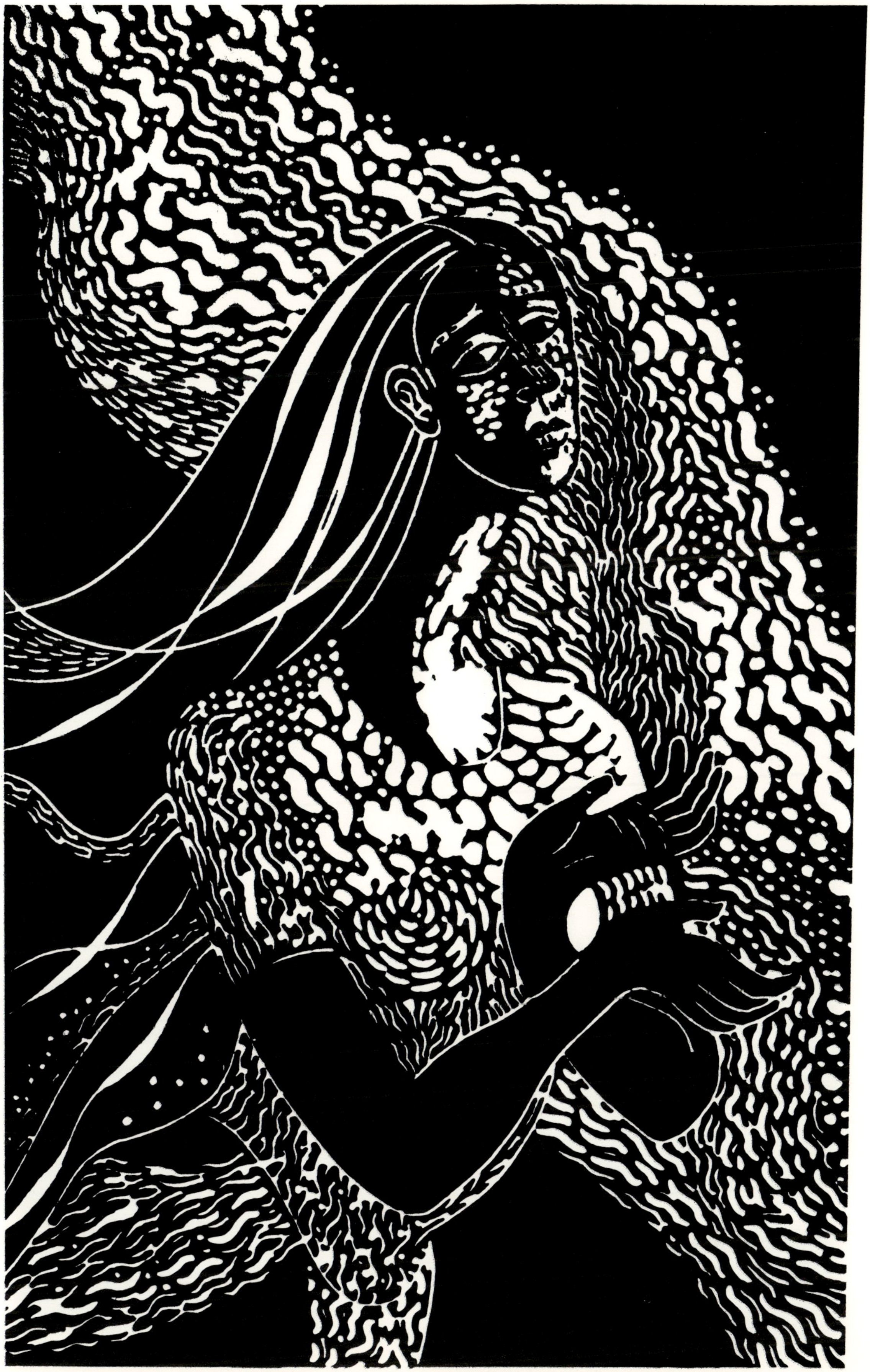

Truth,

Fleeting daughter of Eternity,

And brother Time

Through love

Create reality,

Mind and world of man,

Free.

Seduced,

By thought,

Shadow-child of Time,

The self is made,

Image,

Of security and power.

Struggling, fighting

With itself

To be,

Truth and All,

Corrupting, suffering and building

Hollow shelters

Of pride, anxiety, and hope.

And a mockingbird sings to the sun at dawn

And to the blue flower's tenderness.

Truth and the mockingbird

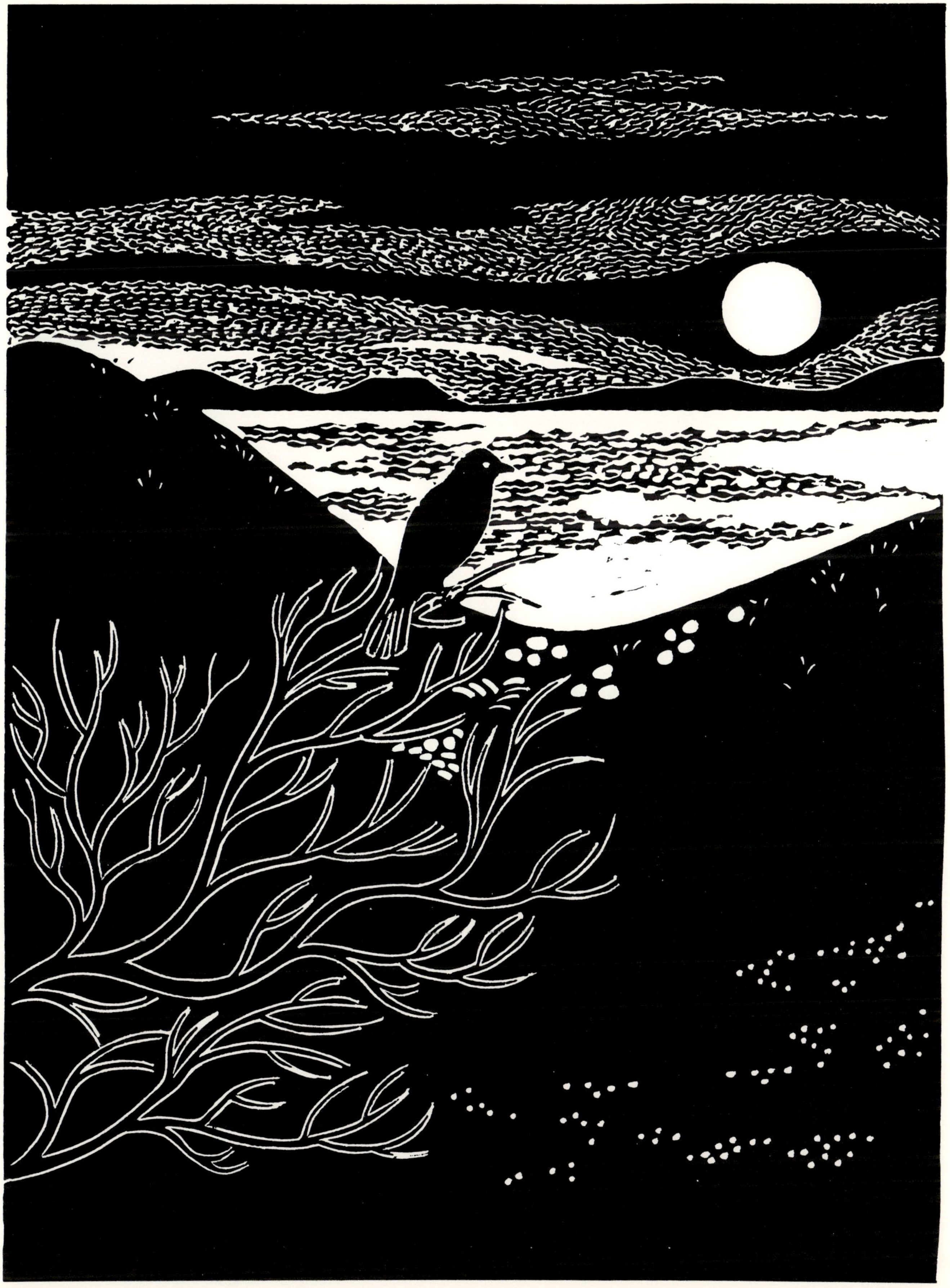

Dreaming is waking

    Waking is dreaming

Waking is not dreaming

    Dreaming is not waking.

Waking and dreaming is one

    Dreaming and waking is not one

Nor is waking and dreaming one

    Nore is waking and dreaming not one.

Dreaming and awake

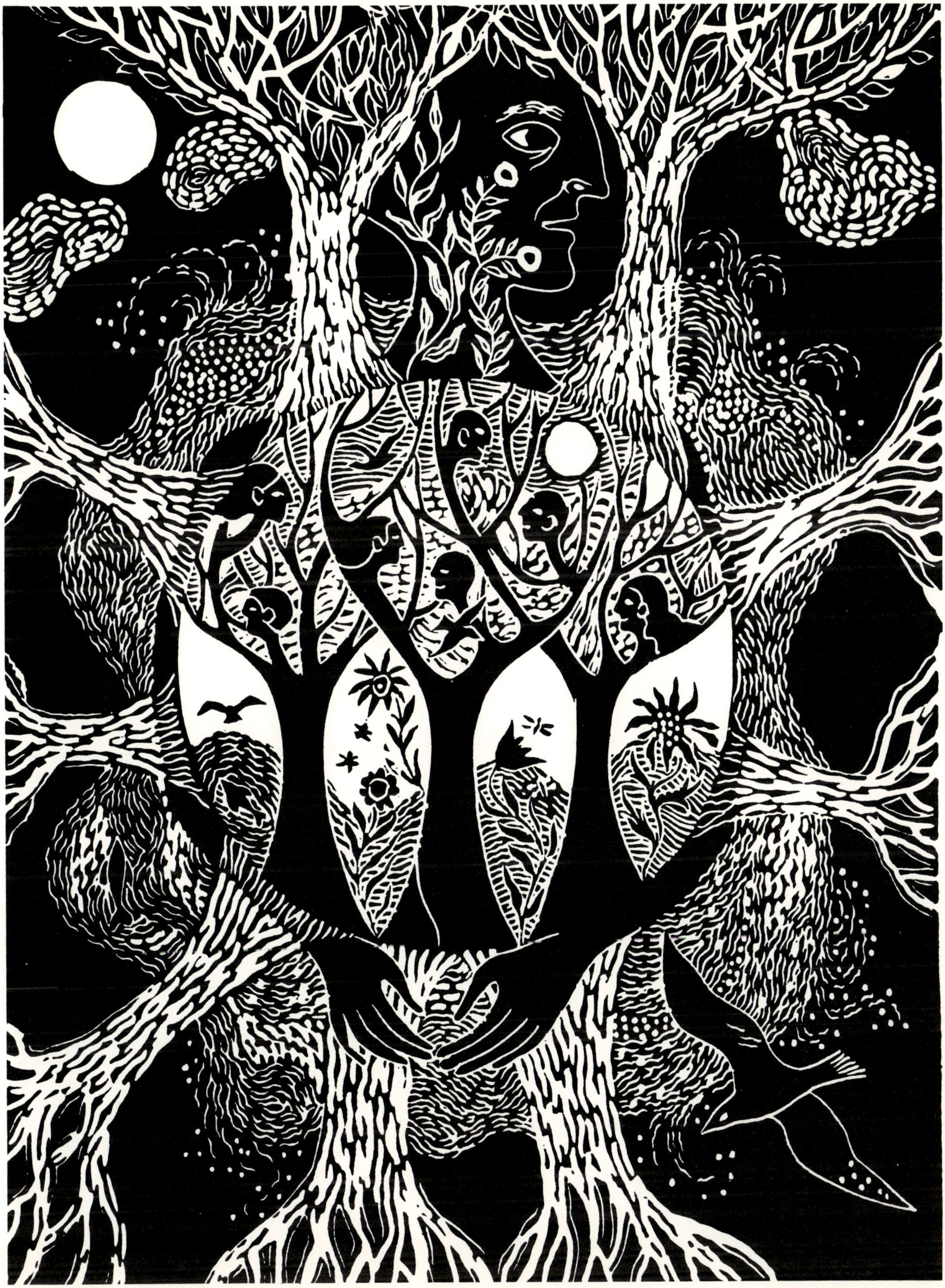

The truth

Of

A reality

Is

The reality

Of

A truth.

The Source—

        IS—

Life and Death,

The Sky

        Bearing

Stars, the Waters,

Earth

        Dreaming

Man,

His dreams and thoughts and feelings,

Man dreaming thinking feeling

Earth,

The Waters,

The Sky, bearing stars,

Life and Death,

Man, Himself—

The Source—

        IS.

The source

There is a dream of the eternal mind

That peoples live and love together

As if they were one kind.

There is a dream of the eternal thought

That neighbors work and dance together

Where they once raged and fought.

There is a dream of the eternal child

That his parents love each other

Instead of making love and vile.

This is our dream.

There also is a dream

That makes a dream come true:

Love and wisdom, dream and fact

Is one and all, and all

    With you.

Dream

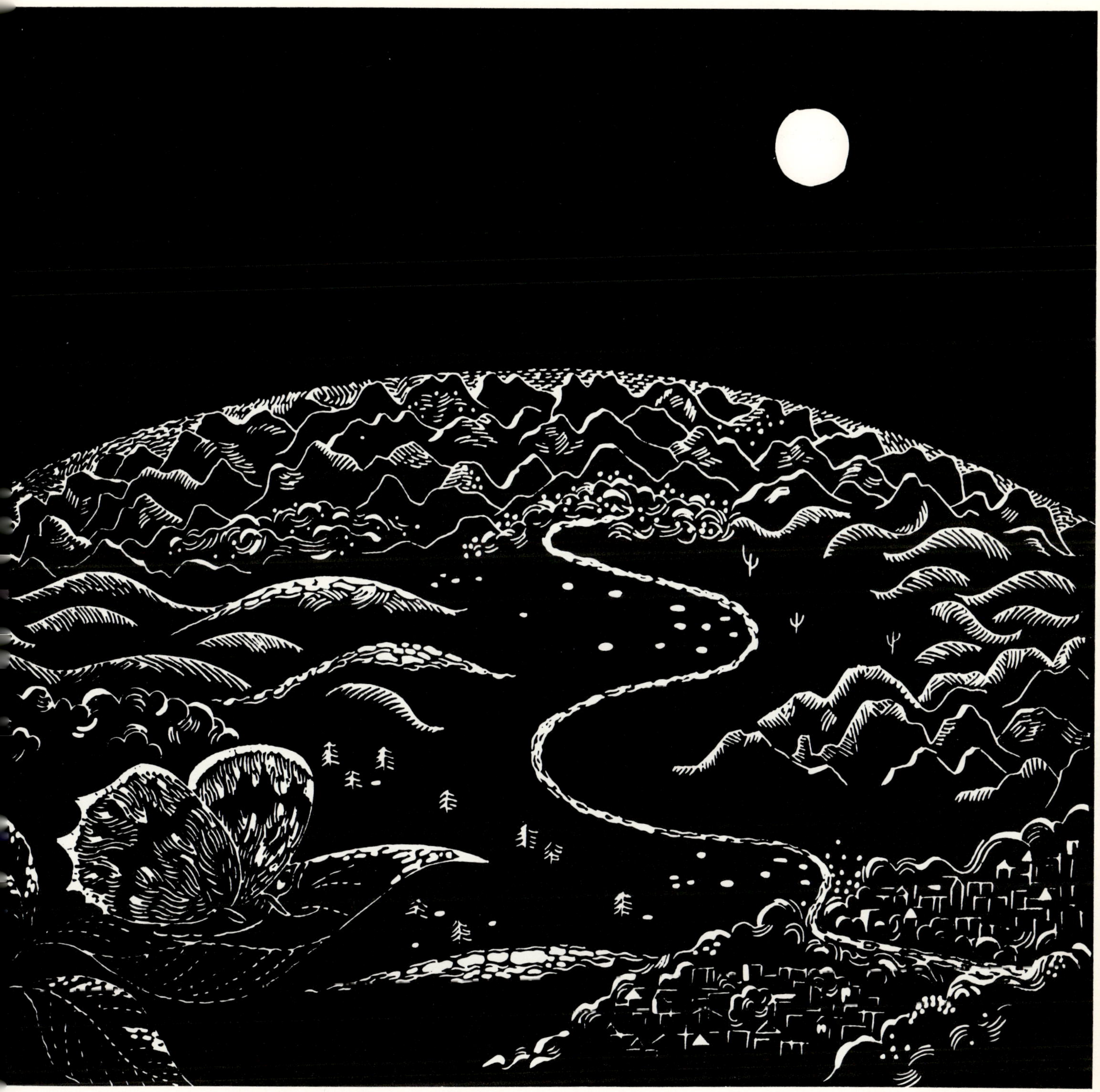

Art/Poetry/Philosophy

MAN,

SHAPER OF THE EARTH,

CONQUEROR OF THE PLANETS,

KNOWS NOT

HIMSELF.

The subject of this book is universal and timeless, a variation of the theme "What is man and what could he be?"

The human struggle to find an answer to his problems is described here through linocuts and poems. Also, through these artistic means the incomprehensible and transcendent nature of man's existence is evoked in a reader-viewer who is able to open up to the urgent appeal of this book. And this very openness might be the "Next Step".